Christmas Crafts
Year-Round

Christmas Crafts Year-Round

60 Great Gifts
*You Can Make
from January
to December*

Holly Boswell

Lark Books
Asheville, North Carolina

EDITOR: **Holly Boswell**

DESIGN AND PRODUCTION: **Chris Bryant**

PHOTOGRAPHY: **Evan Bracken**

ILLUSTRATIONS: **Orrin Lundgren**

Library of Congress Cataloging-in-Publication Data
Boswell, Holly, 1950–
    Christmas crafts year-round : 60 great gifts you can make from
January to December / Holly Boswell.
        p.   cm.
    "A Lark book."
    Includes index.
    ISBN 1-57990-001-1
    1. Christmas decorations.   2. Handicrafts.   I. Title
TT900.C4B665   1997
745.594'12—dc21   97-10660
                                             CIP

10 9 8 7 6 5 4 3 2
First Edition

Published by Lark Books
50 College Street
Asheville, North Carolina 28801
USA

© 1997 Lark Books

Distributed by Random House,Inc., in the United States, Canada, the United Kingdom, Europe, and Asia

Distributed in Australia by Capricorn Link (Australia) Pty Ltd., P.O. Box 6651,
Baulkham Hills Business Centre, NSW 2153, Australia

Distributed in New Zealand by Tandem Press Ltd., 2 Rugby Rd., Birkenhead, Auckland, New Zealand

The written instructions, photographs, designs, patterns, and projects in this volume are intended for the personal use of the reader and may be reproduced for that purpose only. Any other use, especially commercial use, is forbidden under law without written permission of the copyright holder.

Every effort has been made to ensure that all the information in this book is accurate. However, due to differing conditions, tools, and individual skills, the publisher cannot be responsible for any injuries, losses, or other damages that may result from the use of the information in this book.

Printed in Hong Kong
All rights reserved

ISBN 1-57990-001-1

**Christmas Crafts
Year-Round**

Contents

Introduction

THIS BOOK IS ABOUT CHRISTMAS, *but gift giving is truly a year-round proposition. To help offset the spirit of procrastination in all of us, this book lends encouragement for you to create your own special gifts throughout the year. Finding more leisurely opportunities to make gifts for loved ones makes for a much more enjoyable and creative experience—and isn't that what handcrafting should be?*

This is a book you can take off your shelf to find gift ideas for almost any occasion. When it comes to gift giving, whether at birthdays or holidays or any special times, every day is Christmas.

Within these pages, you will find a rich offering of crafts in many media: naturals, woodworking, sewing, jewelry and other decorative pieces. Some projects can be made by beginners, while others require a moderate knowledge of a particular craft. This is a book you can grow into, as you explore your own creativity at whatever level of skill you may feel comfortable. And of course the more of yourself you put into each gift, the more it will be appreciated. These are gift ideas that can lead to many variations and new possibilities.

So as you flip through the pages of this book, looking for that perfect gift for someone special, let it inspire you into new realms. With a little patience, effort, and skill, you can create anything in this book—and more. Gift giving is great fun, and is a year-round endeavor. Celebrate your own spirit of giving through these marvelous crafts.

**Christmas Crafts
Year-Round**

*N*atural
*M*aterials

1

Bundle of Switches

YES, *and a bag of coal, too. This old fashioned inducement for bad little boys and girls to mend their ways may yet serve as a reminder, but also as an attractive conversation piece.*

Materials

- ◆ willow switches
- ◆ sisal or jute twine
- ◆ raffia
- ◆ small canvas bag
- ◆ coal or charcoal
- ◆ silk-vinyl Christmas greenery
- ◆ faux berries
- ◆ pinecones
- ◆ #20 or #21 floral wire

Tools

- ◆ scissors
- ◆ wire cutters
- ◆ hot glue gun

Instructions

1. Fashion the bundle of switches, binding them with sisal or jute twine. A wire loop hanger can be wound into the back side.

2. Insert sprigs of greenery, then berries, in between the switches. Secure them with hot glue.

3. Add a raffia bow to the bag of coal and attach it to the bundle with floral wire. A little of the coal or charcoal can be rubbed onto the bag, or a light mist of black spray paint, to indicate what's inside.

4. Pinecones and more berries can be attached with floral wire and/or hot glue.

Kitchen Swag

THIS *easy-to-make swag lends texture and fragrance to a kitchen. It's also a decorative way to store herbs straight from the garden to be used for cooking. The strand can be varied seasonally or to complement other rooms of the house as well.*

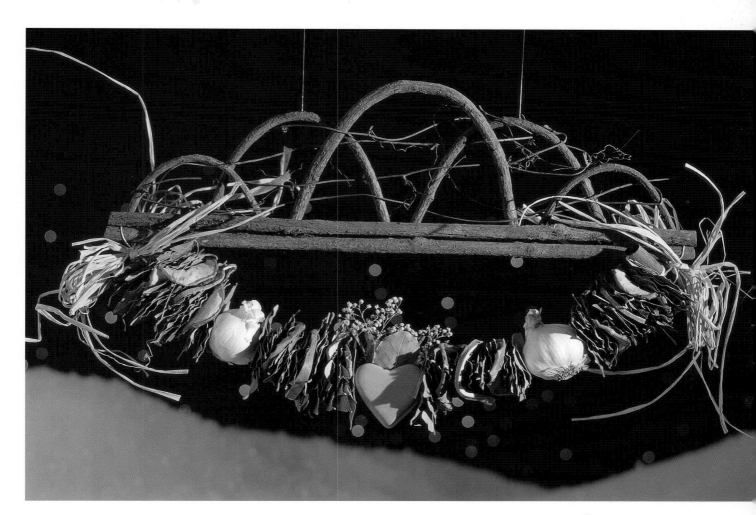

Materials

- 6–10 feet (1.8–3 cm) of grapevine
- small brads
- heavy thread
- bay leaves
- dried fruit slices
- garlic bulbs
- 2 rag bows
- ceramic heart

Tools

- fine-tooth saw
- hammer
- large sewing needle

Instructions

1. Saw two straight pieces of thicker vine to your desired length. Saw five thinner pieces and soak them in a hot tub for a couple of hours.

2. Curve the wet pieces and nail them to the two straight pieces, forming the frame. Tendrils of the vine can be woven through the frame.

3. Tie thread to one end of the frame. Using the needle, thread the hanging items together as you please. A decorative object perforated with a hole, such as this heart, can be strung midway. Tie off the other end.

4. Bows or other tassel materials are tied to the ends for a more finished look.

THIS *simple gift can be prepared quickly on short notice or well in advance, incorporating items gathered year-round from the outdoors. Aloe is wonderful to have handy in the kitchen for treating minor burns.*

loe Vera Basket

Materials

- ◆ aloe plant in 4-inch (10 cm) plastic pot
- ◆ 5-inch (13 cm) wicker basket
- ◆ acrylic craft paints
- ◆ matte finish acrylic glazing medium
- ◆ spray acrylic sealer
- ◆ bits of moss and lichen
- ◆ rocks, shells, driftwood, etc.

Tools

- ◆ paint brush
- ◆ cotton rag

Instructions

1. Brush on a base coat of raw sienna acrylic paint over the basket. Other colors can be substituted to complement whatever found materials you'll be using to cover the soil. Let dry.

2. Spray on a coat of acrylic sealer, and let dry.

3. Prepare a wash of one half glazing medium and one half paint. Use a color lighter than the base color. Brush this over the wicker, allowing it to settle into the cracks. When it's partially dry, lightly wipe down the raised surface with a damp rag. Let dry.

4. Spray on another coat of sealer, and let dry.

5. Cover the potting soil with a layer of dampened ground moss. Arrange your found materials over the top of this. *Note: aloe requires very little watering.*

Kissing Ball

MORE *than just a sprig of mistletoe to kiss beneath, this ball is a celebration of holiday greenery which can be hung conspicuously for even greater effect. It's a gift you can truly give with love.*

Materials

- 3-inch (7.6 cm) styrofoam ball
- moss green spray paint
- 18 inches (45.7 cm) of floral wire (#20–22 gauge)
- narrow red and green satin ribbon
- faux mistletoe with berries
- silk ivy
- moss
- small floral picks with wire
- green floral tape

Tools

- wire cutters
- scissors
- hot glue gun

Instructions

1. First paint the ball green, and let dry.

2. To create a hanger, bend 8 inches (20.3 cm) of wire in half like a hairpin, then push it through the ball. The two stray ends at the bottom are wound around a short twig to prevent it from slipping out.

3. A ribbon loop for hanging can be added to the top of the ball through the wire loop.

4. Bits of moss can be attached to the ball using small wire "hairpins" and/or dabs of hot glue.

5. The mistletoe and ivy are cut into small uniform bunches and secured with wired floral picks, finished with a wrap of floral tape. These are inserted into the ball and secured with a bit of hot glue.

6. Tie one bow of red and green ribbon to the top of the ball, and another to the bottom.

Mussel Shell Wreath

Here's a project you can begin during a summer vacation at the beach.
Perhaps no one will suspect why it is you're gathering shells so deliberately.

Materials

- styrofoam wreath
- acrylic or spray paint to match shells
- shells
- household bleach
- clear acrylic sealer
- ribbon

Tools

- paint brush (unless using spray)
- hot glue gun

Instructions

1. Soak shells overnight in a solution of half bleach and half water. Then dry, and sort for size and shape.

2. Spray or brush paint onto styrofoam wreath form, and let dry.

3. A ribbon loop hanger is hot glued to the top of the wreath.

4. Beginning around the outer edge, attach shells with a lower temperature of hot glue. Overlap the shells as you go. More can be added to fill in with a subsequent layer.

5. Spray the finished wreath with two or three coats of sealer.

6. Tie a bow with ribbon that complements the shells. Attach with hot glue.

Dried Flower Garland

IMAGINE *this glorious creation festooning someone's doorway, or mantel, or mirror. Even in your own home, it would be a gift of beauty to all who visit.*

Materials

- 2 lengths of green clothesline or sash cord
- green floral wire (#26 or #30 gauge)
- dried plants from the garden and/or floral supply store: babies' breath, sweet Annie, asparagus fern, celosia, zinnias, marigolds, strawflowers, rabbit tobacco, statice, and roses

Tools

- wire cutters
- floral shears
- hot glue gun

Instructions

1. If the cords aren't already green, they should be dyed or painted. Tie each one off tautly between two points.

2. Starting at one end, small bunches of dried material (except roses, marigolds and zinnias) are wrapped around the cord with floral wire. Each bunch should overlap the previously wired one, and they all face in the same direction.

3. When both are covered, tie them together so that they face away from each other. Then tie off the entire length between two points.

4. Attach the roses, marigolds and zinnias with hot glue in a pleasing, symmetrical arrangement. More filler, such as babies' breath and statice, can be added as well.

Topiaries

are fun and easy to construct, and make unique decorator gifts for any holiday year-round. Here are just a few designs and techniques to get you started.

Terra-Cotta Topiary

Materials

- terra-cotta pot
- water based craft paints
- water proof tape
- plaster of paris
- 4- to 5-inch (10 to 13 cm) x ⅜-inch (1 cm) diameter wooden dowel
- styrofoam cone
- leftover silk flower heads
- vinyl fruit
- bisque finish
- ribbon

Tools

- paint brushes
- hot glue gun
- small 3d nails or straight pins

Instructions

1. To antique the pot, first brush on a wash of water-thinned moss green paint, and let dry. with a stiff bristle brush, flick on spots of thinned brown paint.

2. Paint the styrofoam cone with terra-cotta colored paint, and let dry.

3. Tape over the hole in the bottom of the pot. Mix the plaster of paris as directed and pour to fill half the pot.

4. Sharpen one end of the dowel and stick it into the base of the cone. Place the other end of the dowel so that the cone rests on the rim of the pot, and let dry.

5. Tint the bisque finish to a terra cotta color with burnt sienna, yellow ochre and white craft paints. Apply the finish as directed to all the silk flower heads, vinyl fruit and ribbon tied into a bow. Let these dry at least 24 hours on a wide screen like chicken wire that will expose the entire surface.

6. Using the hot glue gun and/or nails, begin attaching the largest pieces around the bottom of the cone, and work upwards with progressively smaller pieces. Attach a bow at the bottom.

7. Apply one or two more coats of finish over the entire topiary, and let dry. To complete the effect, brush on a thinned wash of burnt sienna and white paint, let dry, then add a glaze of moss green.

Dried Flower Topiary

Materials

- urn-like vase
- styrofoam cone
- water base craft paints
- water proof tape
- plaster of paris
- 4- to 5-inch (10 to 13 cm) x ⅜-inch (1 cm) diameter wooden dowel
- silk greenery
- dried bay leaves
- bits of moss
- dried flowers (roses, zinnias, marigolds, strawflowers...)
- seed pods and cones
- floral wire
- spray sealer designed for dried flowers

Tools

- paint brush
- hot glue gun
- wire cutters

Instructions

1. Follow steps 2–4 for the terra-cotta project.

2. The dried flowers shown here were gathered from a home garden throughout the summer and dried using the silica-gel in a microwave method. They are attached with floral wire cut and bent into "hairpins" and/or hot glue. The larger objects are generally placed lower, tapering smaller toward the top.

3. Spray the finished piece with sealer. Avoid placing this topiary in direct sunlight which will fade the colors.

Moss Topiary

Materials

- terra-cotta pot
- styrofoam ball
- waterproof tape
- plaster of paris
- straight section of tree limb
- moss green paint
- honeysuckle vine
- lichen
- ground moss and/or green sheet
- floral wire
- white glue
- thick designer craft glue
- seed pods
- mushrooms

Tools

- paint brush
- ⅜-inch (1 cm) drill
- wire cutters
- hot glue gun

Instructions

1. Paint the styrofoam ball moss green, and let dry. The pot can be antiqued using the same process in the terra-cotta topiary, if desired.

2. Drill a hole in the ball to accept the tree limb. Use white glue to secure the limb in this hole.

3. Mix plaster of paris and pour to fill half the pot, with the bottom hole taped over. Position the limb, prop it up and let dry.

4. Wrap honeysuckle vines around the trunk and place lichen over the plaster.

5. After misting the ground moss or green sheet (available at floral supply stores) to make it pliable, use wire cut and bent into "hairpins" to attach it around the ball. Thick glue can be applied first to further secure the moss. The color of the moss can be enhanced by spraying on a mist of green food coloring diluted with water, and can be retouched later in this way if the color fades with age.

6. Attach the pods, mushrooms, more lichens, and even dried insects if you like, using the hairpins and/or hot glue. If you are using natural objects from the woods, place them in a plastic bag, spray with insecticide, seal it and let stand overnight.

Porcelainized Topiary

Materials

- urn-like vase
- water base paints
- water proof tape
- plaster of paris
- 4- to 5-inch (10 to 13 cm) x ³⁄₈-inch (1 cm) diameter wooden dowel
- styrofoam cone
- leftover silk flower heads
- silk greenery
- vinyl fruit
- porcelainizing agent
- spray sealer
- spray gloss

Tools

- paint brushes
- hot glue gun
- small 3d nails or straight pins

Instructions

1. This project follows the same basic steps as the terra-cotta. Depending on the vase you find, you may want to add an antique finish. Paint the cone moss green, and let dry.

2. Install the cone with the dowel using plaster of paris as before.

3. After attaching all floral materials to the cone, apply the porcelainizing agent as directed.

4. Brush on a white-wash glaze of thinned craft paint, and let dry.

5. Apply a coat of spray sealer, let dry, then finish with a spray gloss.

Christmas Crafts
Year-Round

Found
Objects
2

Santa's Sleigh

A PERFECT *centerpiece for the holidays, this decorative gift will achieve heirloom status as it is brought out and displayed for years to come. You can even personalize it with tiny name tags on the packages.*

Materials

- purchased wooden sleigh
- acrylic paints
- black antiquing glaze
- crackle finish
- gray spray paint
- miniature old fashioned toys, ornaments, bells, lanterns, etc.
- sisal trees and wreaths
- tiny blocks of wood or styrofoam
- faded wrapping paper
- Victorian stickers and/or clipped images
- bits of twine, yarn and cord
- household bleach
- white glue
- glass glitter or laundry detergent granules

Tools

- paint brushes
- old toothbrush
- fine sandpaper
- hot glue gun
- scissors

Instructions

1. Sleighs like this can be found at many craft or toy stores. Paint it dull red if it isn't already, and let dry.

2. Splatters of thinned, black glaze are flicked on with a toothbrush for the antique effect. Let dry.

3. Worn areas are simulated using sandpaper. Gray spray paint can be applied lightly for a dusty, aged look. Apply crackle finish according to the directions to complete the effect.

4. The miniature toys, etc. can be found in craft stores, antique shops and Christmas specialty stores. You may have some stashed away and forgotten in your own attic. Use the faded paper, Victorian images and bits of twine to wrap the blocks of wood to create the packages. To age the sisal items or any fabric pieces, dip them briefly in diluted bleach.

5. Gather up all the contents for the sleigh and start arranging them. Once you've decided their positions, attach them with hot glue, beginning with the larger pieces. Keep proportion and scale in mind as you go.

6. The exterior of the sleigh can be decorated with small bells, lanterns and sisal wreaths.

7. The entire piece can now be further aged with a mist of gray spray paint. Faux snow can be added sparsely by applying patches of white glue, then sprinkling on the glitter or soap flakes. After drying, blow away the excess.

all Basket

ISN'T *it ever so helpful to have a place to put
all those incoming Christmas cards? Here's
an easy gift you can make that will be
used and appreciated for years.*

Materials

- ◆ purchased wall basket
- ◆ Christmas fabric
- ◆ poster board
- ◆ spray adhesive
- ◆ a special Christmas card or other graphic

Tools

- ◆ scissors

Instructions

1. Cut a liner out of the poster board to fit the interior of the basket and the upper wall panel.

2. Cut this same shape out of Christmas fabric, with a ½-inch (1.3 cm) margin added all around. Spray the interior surfaces of the liner, and the backside of the fabric, with adhesive. Press together, smoothing out the wrinkles. Spray the backside and fabric margins, then fold the fabric around to the back.

3. Install this liner by spraying the interior basket surfaces and the backsides of the liner, then pressing into place. This could also be installed with a hot glue gun or a needle and thread.

4. The Christmas card or graphic is attached very simply using any of these same processes.

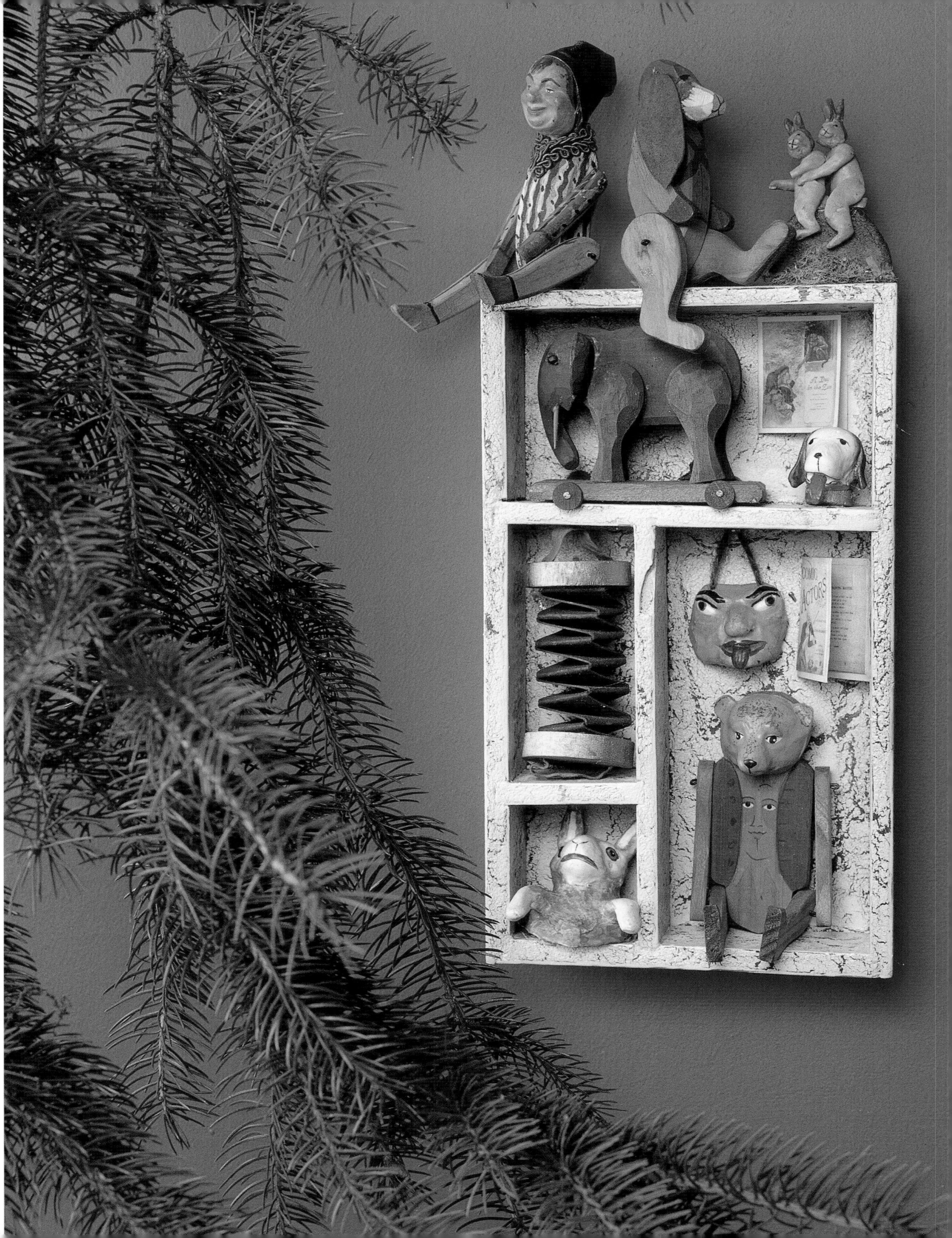
COMIC
ACTORS

Shadow Box

THIS *is a fabulous opportunity to create something*
that you can personalize as a special memento.
Most anyone would be delighted to display
such a piece in their home.

Materials

- purchased shadow box
- acrylic paints
- crackle finish
- dark antiquing glaze or gray spray paint
- miniature old fashioned toys, ornaments, jewelry, etc.
- old fashioned images on paper scraps
- white glue

Tools

- paint brushes
- old toothbrush
- hot glue gun

Instructions

1. If you can't find a box or type tray like this at a craft store or antique shop, it can be constructed rather easily out of thin panels of pine or plywood. Cut to fit, and join with glue and small nails.

2. Brush on a base coat of paint, and let dry.

3. Apply a liberal coat of crackle finish. When it has partially dried to a tacky finish, apply a coat of paint in a contrasting color to the base coat. Let shrink and dry.

4. Further antiquing can be accomplished by splattering dark glaze or misting with gray paint, as described in the Santa's Sleigh project.

5. The miniature toys, etc. can be found in craft stores and Christmas specialty shops, or perhaps you've already collected a few over the years. Arrange them in the box and secure them with hot glue.

6. Images on paper scraps can be affixed with white glue. Edges may be cut or torn. Further antiquing can be done by "flyspeck" splattering of diluted paint with a toothbrush.

**Christmas Crafts
Year-Round**

Dolls and Figurines

3

Antique Doll

LET *us introduce you to Margaret. She's a 1-foot 7-inch redhead—an Early American girl with a long shelf life. Perhaps you can give her a new life, and a new home.*

Materials

- 1 foot (30.5 cm) of sturdy wire
- cardboard for 15½" (39.4 cm) cone
- paper mache mix
- ½ yard (46 cm) cotton print fabric
- ⅜" (1 cm) satin ribbon
- ½" (1.3 cm) lace trim
- 1½" (4 cm) lace trim
- ⅓ yard (30.5 cm) muslin
- masking tape
- thread
- aluminum foil
- gesso
- acrylic paints
- spray sealer
- antiquing medium
- wet/dry fine sand paper

Tools

- sewing equipment
- sculpting tools
- paint brushes

Instructions

1. Create a cone from cardboard, taping it together with masking tape. (A)

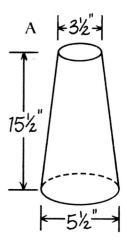

A ⊢3½"⊣

15½"

⊢5½"⊣

2. Crumple aluminum foil into an armature for the head and neck. The neck should be ¾" (2 cm) long and 1¼" (3 cm) in diameter. The head should be 1½" (4 cm) wide and 2" (5 cm) oval. Attach these with masking tape to the top of the cone.

3. Wrap the heavy wire once around the top of the cone, leaving 6½" (16.5 cm) at each side to support the arms and hands. (B)

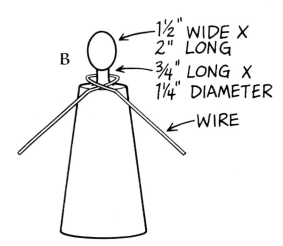

B 1½" WIDE X 2" LONG

¾" LONG X 1¼" DIAMETER

WIRE

4. Cover the cardboard cone with a ¼" (.6 cm) layer of paper mache. Then cover the foil neck and head, and smoothe with the sculpting tools. Build up the forehead area with paper mache, then blend and smoothe. Add a triangle shape for the nose, two balls for the cheeks, then blend and smooth. Build up the chin area, blend again, but be sure to leave the eye area indented. Add a layer of hair, and texture it with the sculpting tools.

5. Create simple spoon shaped hands with 1½" (4 cm) long ovals of paper mache that are ⅝" (1.6 cm) wide. Spear these onto the wire arms so that 5" (13 cm) of arm is still exposed.

6. Allow head and hands to dry thoroughly. Sand well with the sandpaper. Paint on a coat of gesso for added smoothness. For a more antique appearance, use ivory rather than fleshtone paint for the skin. Paint the hair and facial features. Let dry. Spray on the sealer. Let dry. Apply antiquing medium.

7. For the underskirt, cut a 12" x 18" (30.5 x 45.7 cm) rectangle of muslin. Stitch the short sides together with a ¼" (.6 cm) seam allowance. Turn under the bottom edge ¼" (.6 cm) and hem. Sew 1½" (4 cm) lace trim around the bottom edge of the underskirt.

8. Turn under a ¼" (.6 cm) of the top edge and run a gather stitch around it. Place the underskirt on the doll and tighten the gather at her waist. Tack it down. The finished length of the underskirt should reach to the bottom of the doll base.

9. For the dress, fold the printed fabric in half, then fold it in half the other way. (C and D) You will then have a fold at the top and a fold at the right edge. Place the pattern (E) on the fabric with the top sleeve edge and the center of the dress on the folds. Cut it out, stitch up the outside skirt and bottom arm seams using a ¼" (.6 cm) seam allowance. Turn it to the right side.

10. Turn under the neck edge ¼" (.6 cm) and run a gather stitch. Place the dress on the doll, pull in the gathers and tack it down.

11. Do the same around the sleeve edges, and tack them down at the wrists.

12. Hem the skirt bottom ¾" (2 cm) shorter than the doll so that ¾" (2 cm) of the petticoat shows.

13. Stitch ½" (1.3 cm) lace around the neck.

14. Tie satin ribbon at the waist.

Note: Fabrics can be stained with tea for a more antique appearance.

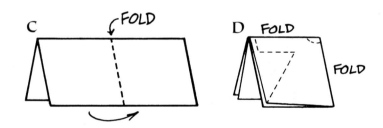

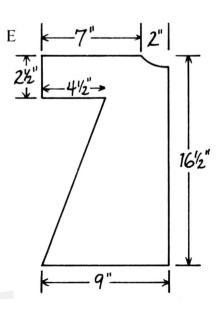

Fabric Mache Angel

WHAT *would Christmas be without an angel? In fact, angels have become quite popular year-round. This one has a hollow body and can sit atop the tree, bestowing her blessings from on high.*

Materials

- ◆ wool doll hair
- ◆ 1½" (4 cm) wooden head bead
- ◆ purchased gold wings
- ◆ purchased 3-inch (8 cm) trumpet
- ◆ ⅜" (1 cm) gold braid trim
- ◆ ⅓ yard (30.5 cm) cotton fabric
- ◆ cardboard for 8-inch (2 cm) cone
- ◆ fabric stiffener
- ◆ thread masking tape
- ◆ white glue
- ◆ paint or markers

Tools

- ◆ scissors
- ◆ sewing needles or machine
- ◆ paint brushes
- ◆ hot glue gun

Instructions

1. Make a cone from cardboard 8" (20 cm) tall with a 3-inch (7.6 cm) diameter base. Tape it together with masking tape.

2. Glue wooden bead to top of cone with hot glue.

3. Following patterns A and B, cut fabric, adding a ¼-inch (.6 cm) seam allowance at sleeves and sides. Sew together under sleeves and down sides.

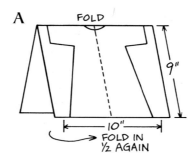
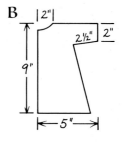

4. Dip it into fabric stiffener and wring out the excess. Run a gather stitch around the neck, turning underedge ¼" (.6 cm). Place the robe on the doll and pull the gather stitch until tight, then tie it off. Tack sleeves together at the wrists in front of the doll. Arrange folds in the robe as desired. Let dry.

5. Glue gold braid around neck and at the bottom of the robe.

6. Skin tones for the face can be applied as a wash of half acrylic and half water. Add facial features with markers or paint.

7. Affix the wings with hot glue.

8. Affix the wool hair with white glue, then the gold braid halo.

9. Hot glue or stitch the trumpet to a sleeve edge.

Egg Head Santa

THIS *whimsical figure could adorn a mantelpiece, be featured in a dining table centerpiece, or find its way to some special nook in a child's bedroom. It's even light enough to hang as a tree ornament.*

Materials

- 4-inch (10 cm) styrofoam egg
- instant paper mache mix
- acrylic paints
- spray sealer
- antiquing medium

Tools

- scupting tools
- paint brushes

Instructions

1. Cover the styrofoam egg with a thin ⅛"–¼" (.3 – .6 cm) layer of paper mache mix. Smooth well.

2. Add a rectangle of paper mache to the forehead and create wrinkles using sculpting tool.

3. Add a triangle of paper maché for the nose and blend to shape with the tool.

4. Add two circles for cheeks and blend with tool, keeping eye areas indented.

5. Add the beard and texture it with tool.

6. Add a long triangle for the tail of the stocking cap.

7. Add the mustache, and a ball on the end of the cap.

8. After allowing it to dry thoroughly, paint the figure as shown.

9. After the paint dries, spray it with sealant.

10. The antiquing medium is applied last. (Follow directions on container.)

11. To use as a tree ornament, insert a paper clip half way into the top of the head and bend.

Santa Americana

THOMAS NAST *would be proud to see this flag-waving Santa, proving what a cultural icon he has become. This distinctive piece would add the perfect accent to most any old fashioned Christmas decor.*

Materials

4" (10 cm) styrofoam ball
1½" (4 cm) styrofoam ball
2 toothpicks
paper mache mix
acrylic paints
spray sealer
antiquing medium
paper flag ribbon
2-inch (5 cm) wooden stick

Tools

sculpting tools
paint brushes
white glue

Instructions

1. Join the two balls with two toothpicks.

2. Cover them with a ⅜" (1 cm) layer of paper mache.

3. Make 4" (10 cm) long paper mache coils for arms and add them below the neck, bending them at the elbows. Smoothe and blend with sculpting tools.

4. Add 1" (2.5 cm) long ovals for mittens.

5. Insert wooden stick into right mitten.

6. Add a triangle to the face for a nose, and two balls for cheeks. Smoothe and blend with tools.

7. Add the red portion of the cap to the head.

8. Using sculpting tools to create texture, add beard and hair, then the mustache.

9. Similarly, add fur trim to hat, sleeves and edges of robe.

10. Let dry thoroughly.

11. Paint the figure as shown, using a fine brush for details. Let dry thoroughly.

12. Spray on the sealer, and let dry.

13. Apply antiquing medium as directed on the label.

14. Glue a panel of flag ribbon to the stick, or paint your own on heavy paper.

Christmas Crafts
Year-Round

Surface Design

Gift Wrap and Tags

TIRED *of the same old gift wrappings? Want to do something special—not just for Christmas, but for any occasion? Try these out, then let your imagination carry you.*

Materials

- ◆ brown craft paper
- ◆ lunch bags
- ◆ natural and found objects
- ◆ dried or silk flowers
- ◆ raffia
- ◆ organza ribbon
- ◆ paint

Tools

- ◆ scissors
- ◆ tape
- ◆ hot glue gun
- ◆ paint brushes
- ◆ paint pens
- ◆ hole punch

Instructions

1. Cut craft paper to size needed for gift. Use paint pens and/or paint with brushes to create any designs you wish. Children can do this, too. Let dry, then wrap.

2. Paper bags can be painted or left plain. Insert gift, fold over twice at top, then punch a hole or two to tie closed with raffia or ribbon. Add handmade tag with ribbon or hot glue.

3. For tags, cut brown or other colored cardboard to desired size. Use glue gun to attach pinecones, dried flowers, artificial fruit, or other natural or found objects. Use paint pens to label.

Decorative Balls

THIS *project has countless variations and is simple enough for a child to make. It's also an opportunity to give something that you can personalize.*

Materials

- ◆ purchased styrofoam balls covered with satin thread
- ◆ scraps of lace, braid, ribbon, loomed beadwork
- ◆ sequins, small beads
- ◆ straight pins

Tools

- ◆ scissors
- ◆ hot glue gun (optional)

Instructions

1. Simply cut a length of lace or other material to fit around the ball with a slight overlap.

2. Insert each pin through a bead and/or sequin before using it to attach the band of lace to the ball. Hot glue may be helpful at times.

3. One popular variation of this project is to incorporate small cutouts of photos from school portraits or elsewhere. All sorts of objects can be utilized.

Painted Garden Set

A WONDERFUL *gift idea for both indoor and outdoor gardeners year-round. You can even throw in some seed packets and potting soil.*

Materials

- terra-cotta pots
- garden gloves
- garden picks
- acrylic paints
- acrylic gel medium
- gesso (primer)

Tools

- paint brush

Instructions

Flower pots:

1. Prime the entire outside and bottom with gesso. Let dry.
2. Paint random patterns over the entire surface. These patterns were outlined with a darker color for effect. Let dry.
3. Seal with acrylic gel medium.

Garden gloves and picks:

1. The gloves can be painted with acrylic or fabric paints. Your color scheme will tie these into the set even if the pattern is different. No sealer is required.
2. The picks can be found in most craft stores, or easily constructed out of light plywood and dowels. Give them a base coat of differing colors. Let dry.
3. Paint patterns all over, but leave an open panel where the name of the plant can be written. Let dry.
4. Coat entirely with acrylic gel medium to seal.

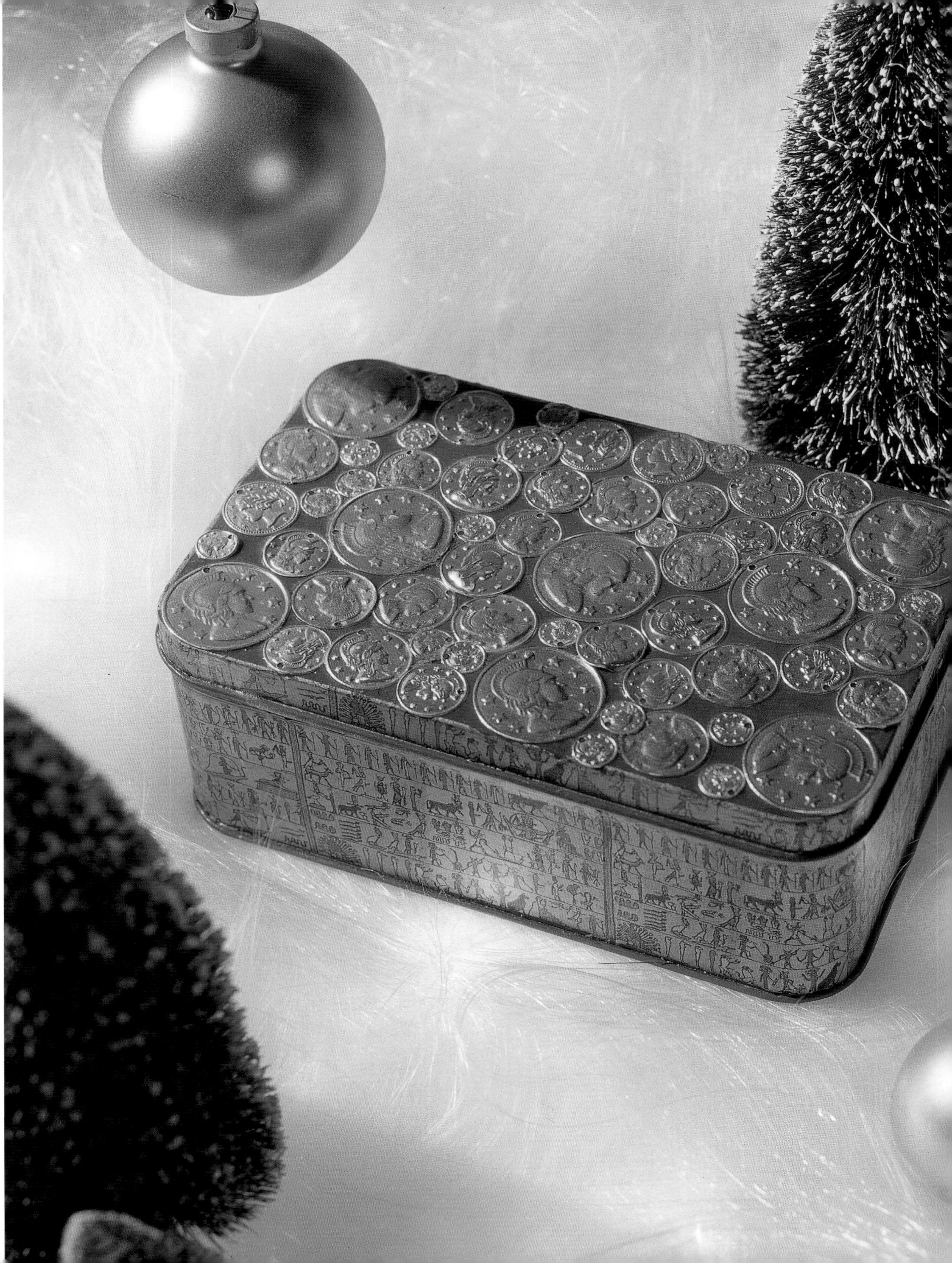

oin Box

PICTURE *this decorative box, not out in the snow,
but on someone's dresser or a coffee table or mantelpiece.
Then imagine what might be put inside...*

Materials

- tin box with lid
- spray red-oxide metal primer
- gold leaf adhesive size
- tacky glue or liquid plastic solder
- coins or faux coins
- powdered graphite lubricant
- metallic tissue paper
- spray glue
- craft felt

Tools

- a soft rag

Instructions

1. Spray the box inside and out with red primer, and let dry. Use as many coats as necessary to cover any images already on the tin.

2. Apply gold leaf size over sides and lid as directed. When it reaches the appropriate degree of tackiness, press the metallic paper on, one surface at a time, with fingers and a rag.

3. Apply a coat of tacky glue or liquid solder over the top of the lid. Press the coins into place, then wipe off the excess glue. Let dry.

4. Rub the graphite all over the lid so that it settles into the spaces between the coins. Clean the excess off of the tops of the coins. Let dry.

5. Cut felt to line the interior of the box. Attach it using spray adhesive, which is applied to both surfaces being joined.

ecorative Candles

SEE *how quick and easy it is to transform ordinary candles into holiday gifts that will be enjoyed throughout the season.*

Materials

for white candle
- bugle beads
- glitter
- white glue

for round candle
- gold braid and bow
- small gold beads
- ½-inch (1.3 cm) straight pins

for green candle
- shiny stars
- glitter
- white glue

for red candle
- Battenburg lace
- narrow white ribbon
- small white beads
- ½-inch (1.3 cm) straight pins

Instructions

White candle:

1. Place candle in a 250-degree oven for a few minutes to soften the surface.

2. While it's heating, spread bugle beads out on a sheet of tin foil. Roll the candle over the beads firmly to get them embedded.

3. Mix a solution of white glue, a little water and some glitter. Rub it over the candle to add sparkle and secure the bugle beads.

Round candle:

1. Cut gold braid to fit around the candle with a slight overlap.

2. Insert each pin through a small bead before pinning the braid around the candle. Position the pins in a pleasing pattern.

3. Tie a bow and pin it to cover the overlap.

Green candle:

1. Glue the stars to the candle in a pleasing pattern.

2. Using the glue and glitter mixture described for the white candle, rub streaked patterns around the stars.

Red candle:

1. Insert each pin through a small bead before pinning the lace to the candle. Create a pattern that is suited to the lace you use.

2. Tie a bow and pin it to cover the overlap.

Tin Ornaments

EACH year we give and receive so many Christmas cards—some of them quite special that we want to keep. Here's a great way to recycle these cards into keepsake ornaments for the tree.

Materials

- ◆ lids from tin cans
- ◆ old Christmas cards
- ◆ spray sealer

Tools

- ◆ felt tip pen
- ◆ paper
- ◆ ruler
- ◆ vise (or pliers)
- ◆ hammer

Instructions

1. To divide the lid into equal sides, stand it on edge on a piece of paper. Mark with the pen on the lid and paper where they touch. Then roll the lid like a wheel (careful, it's sharp) until the mark touches the paper again. Use a ruler to draw a line between the two marks.

2. Measure the distance (a metric scale is easier to divide). Divide this circumference by the number of sides you want, and mark the line at those points (e.g. 5, 10, 15 & 20 for a 4-sided ornament).

3. Roll the lid along the line and mark it to match the line marks on paper. Draw lines connecting the dots on the lid using a ruler.

4. Clamp one edge of the lid in a vise with the jaws along the line. Bend it to a right angle. Continue around and you will have made a shape with equal sides.

5. Use the lid as a guide for cutting out an image from a Christmas card. Place the image inside the lid, then bend the edges over it.

6. Punch a hole for a hanging hook using a small nail and a hammer.

7. Spray lightly with sealer to protect the image over the years.

Watering Can and Seed Box

HERE'S *a very easy way to create a unique gift for any budding horticulturist—even a child. Add a spade and some seed packets, and they'll have a complete starter set.*

Materials

- tin watering can
- tin box
- old seed packets
- spray metal primer
- spray enamel
- decoupage medium (matte finish)
- polyurethane or spray acrylic sealer

Tools

- scissors
- paint brush

Instructions

1. Spray one or more coats of primer onto both objects, allowing them to dry between coats.

2. Spray one or more coats of enamel, in your choice of color, and let dry.

3. Cut to size the seed packets, or color photocopy images of your choice, and spray them with acrylic sealer front and back. Let dry.

4. Affix with decoupage medium, according to instructions, smoothing out air pockets and wrinkles. Apply subsequent coats as directed.

5. Apply polyurethane or acrylic sealer.

$\mathcal{P}$et Placemats

HOW *better to gift someone than to give something to their pet? It's a great opportunity to express your caring for those they care for. Plus, this is something they won't have.*

Materials

- ◆ ½ yard (46 cm) primed canvas
- ◆ gesso
- ◆ acrylic paints
- ◆ acrylic gel medium

Tools

- ◆ paint brushes
- ◆ sponge
- ◆ scissors or pinking shears

Instructions

1. Cut the canvas to your desired shape and size. You might consider a square, oval or rectangle shape.

2. Paint both sides of the canvas with gesso. Let dry.

3. For the background, tile can be painted or a texture can be daubed on with a sponge using successive colors. White, grey and blue were used here. For tile, mark off a grid of squares. Paint one color (peach here) from the left side of each tile and white from the right, blending them into the center. Let dry. A thin line of grout is then painted over either background, and let dry.

4. Use the photo as a guide to copy the figures, sketching them lightly before painting them. Add shadows with grey. Let dry.

5. Coat entirely with the gel medium to seal the paint.

Painted Chair

A WHIMSICAL *approach to decorating furniture for a child's room or as an accent piece most anywhere. Tables, bureaus, headboards and lamps are all fair game. Spanish flash cards are the motif used here, but the possibilities are endless.*

Materials
- furniture
- acrylic paints
- polyurethane sealer

Tools
- sanding implements
- paint brushes
- sponge or rag
- felt tip marker

Instructions

1. Sand off any glossy paint or finish before beginning.

2. Paint on a background color. This can be textured by daubing on a second color with a sponge or crumpled rag. Let dry.

3. Different colored rectangles are then painted as backgrounds for the flash card images, and let dry.

4. As you paint each image, leave space at the bottom of the card to write the word, which can be written more easily with a felt tip marker than a paint brush. Let dry.

5. Seal the entire surface with polyurethane.

**Christmas Crafts
Year-Round**

Woodworking

5

Ornamental Box

MOST any wood-worker will have fun turning out a piece like this once in a while. It's made entirely from the kind of scrap that accumulates in a woodshop, or around other larger projects.

Materials

- any planking, 1 inch thick or less
- picture moulding and/or window trim
- old legs, staircase ballisters or chair spokes
- large wooden bead or knob
- finishing nails
- 2-inch wood screws
- carpenters glue
- leftover paints

Tools

- table saw
- mitre saw
- hammer
- screwdriver
- sanding implements
- paint brushes

Instructions

1. The actual dimensions of your box will be determined by the size of scrap you have, and your own inclinations. Rip cut enough planking for four equal panels, then miter-cut the ends to form the sides of the box. These can be joined with glue using picture frame clamps or even taped in place to dry. Seams may be reinforced after drying with brads.

2. Cut a base to match the outer dimensions of the box. Cut four legs the same length and attach to the base with glue and screws, countersunk.

3. Glue and nail the base to the sides.

4. Cut a lid and a liner. The lid can be a little larger than the box, and the liner should fit cleanly inside the box. Glue and nail the liner to the center of the lid.

5. This is where it gets fun. Play with your scraps of ornamental trim to dress up the box however you like. These will be mitre cut, then glued and nailed into place. A top knob may need to be reinforced with a screw.

6. Sand all the edges, then paint as you wish.

FISHES *are so diverse and beautiful, they offer wonderful decorative motifs. This project is merely a beginning point for you to explore their amazing array of forms, and how they might be incorporated into varying decor.*

Fish Carving

Materials

- 1 x 12 x 36-inch pine, or whatever size you like
- carbon paper
- latex paints
- purchased "crackle finish" or carpenters glue
- satin or dull varnish

Tools

- band, scroll or sabre saw
- wood rasp
- palm sander or sanding block
- dremel tool
- ½-inch sanding drum
- paint brushes

Instructions

1. Choose your favorite drawing or picture of a fish, and enlarge it to your desired size. Transfer this drawing, through carbon paper, to the wood.

2. Cut the outline of the fish, then rasp the edges to the proper contour. Rough sand it. Use the dremel tool and the ½-inch sanding drum to cut in the eyes, gills and fins, then bevel these cuts. Finish sanding with fine sandpaper.

3. Paint the figure with latex (or acrylic) paints.

4. For a weathered appearance, first paint with an off-white latex, and let dry. Then coat with "crackle finish," or diluted carpenters glue (equal proprtions of water and glue), and let dry. Then paint the colors, and let dry. Varnish may then be applied to seal.

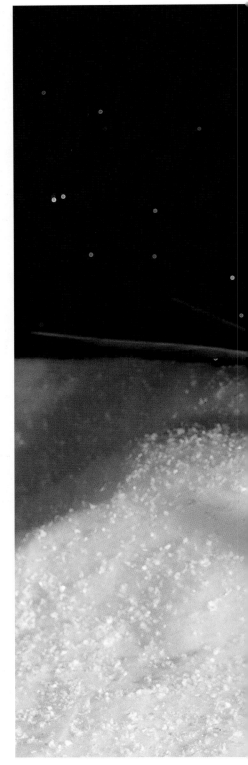

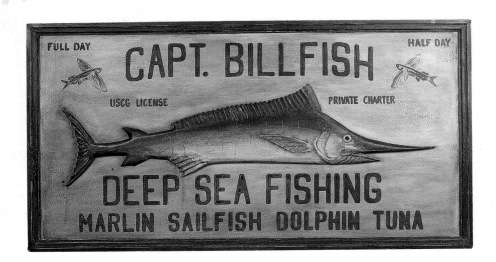

ain Stick

RAIN STICKS *can be found in most of the places where bamboo grows. They are used as musical instruments in Africa, and as a ceremonial instrument preceding the rainy seasons in Central and South America.*

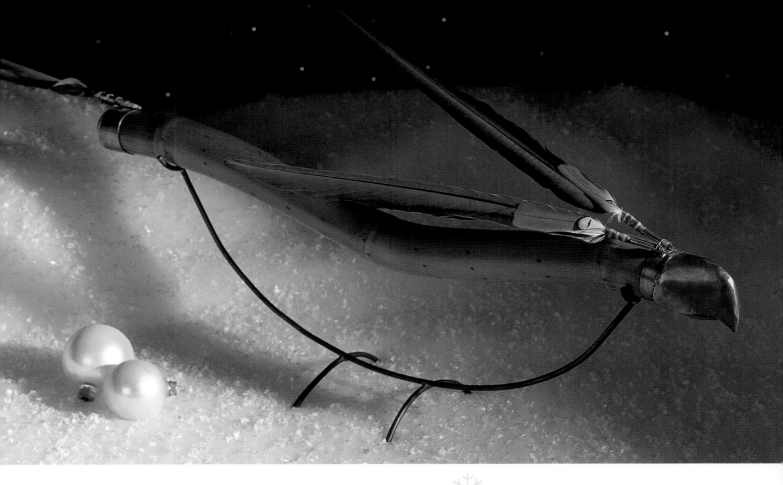

Materials

- 1½–2-inch diameter bamboo, well seasoned
- bamboo skewers
- 2 corks
- 1–2 cups of aquarium gravel or beads
- decorative embellishments of your choice

Tools

- ½-inch rebar
- $^{7}/_{64}$-inch drill bit
- drill
- razor knife

Instructions

1. Use a straight length of rebar to gently knock away each membrane dividing the bamboo sections. Other tubular materials, preferably natural, can be used in place of bamboo.

2. Imagine or lightly draw a spiral line around the cylinder that is parallel and spaced 1½–2 inches apart. Drill holes ½–¾ inches apart along this line. Depending on the size of your skewers, the drill bit may need to be adjusted. It should be slightly smaller than the skewer.

3. Shave the square edges of the skewers with a razor knife for a snug fit. Insert skewers into the holes, randomnly varying the depth of insertion which will create a better tonal quality. Cut each skewer flush using the knife.

4. Trim a large cork to fit snugly into one end of the cylinder. Insert it flush, then drill three equidistant holes laterally into the cork through the banboo. Insert skewers to hold cork in place.

5. Add a cup or more of gravel, depending on the length of your cylinder. Experiment with beads, seeds, or other materials, as well as the amount, before sealing the other end in the same manner.

6. Decorate as you desire. Copper end caps are used here, along with feathers and crystals. Carving or woodburning the stick is another way to personalize it as a gift.

Swan Carving

SWANS *are mythical beings. Their grace and beauty could adorn many a space. This project provides an opportunity for you to share this magic with another.*

Materials

- 1 x 12 x 17-inch knot-free pine
- 5 feet of ⅝-inch metal band and fastening clip (from lumber yard)
- (2) 1-inch wood screws
- a picture hanger
- brown stain
- acrylic paints
- spray sealer
- carbon paper
- sandpapers, a range of grades
- antiquing medium (black)

Tools

- saber or jigsaw
- wood carving tools
- paint brushes
- drill
- screwdriver
- pliers

Instructions

1. Using the illustration below, trace the outline and carving pattern through carbon paper onto the wood.

2. Using a sabre or jigsaw, cut out the entire swan with its base.

3. The first carving step is called grounding. Outline the area to be lowered with a V-shaped carving tool. Then use the chisel to remove the neighboring wood. Do this in layers, utilizing whatever tools prove effective to the wood.

4. Use a knife blade to round off the outside edges of the swan, especially the beak and neck ring.

5. The textured effect on the base is achieved using the V-shaped tool. Carve horizontally along the base repeatedly until you reach your desired depth.

6. After carving, sand with a progression of finer papers.

7. Stain the entire piece brown, using brushes and rags. Let dry.

8. Paint the swan and base with acrylics. Let dry.

9. Lightly sand over the paint to reveal the brown stain, achieving an antique appearance.

10. Spray with sealer.

11. Use the black antiquing medium to further the effect, especially in the deeper areas.

12. Wrap the banding material around the swan to form a hoop, fastening it with the banding clip, using pliers.

13. Place the swan inside the hoop and, with a metal drill, create holes to insert two screws on opposite sides of the base.

14. Affix the picture hanging hook to the upper back of the swan.

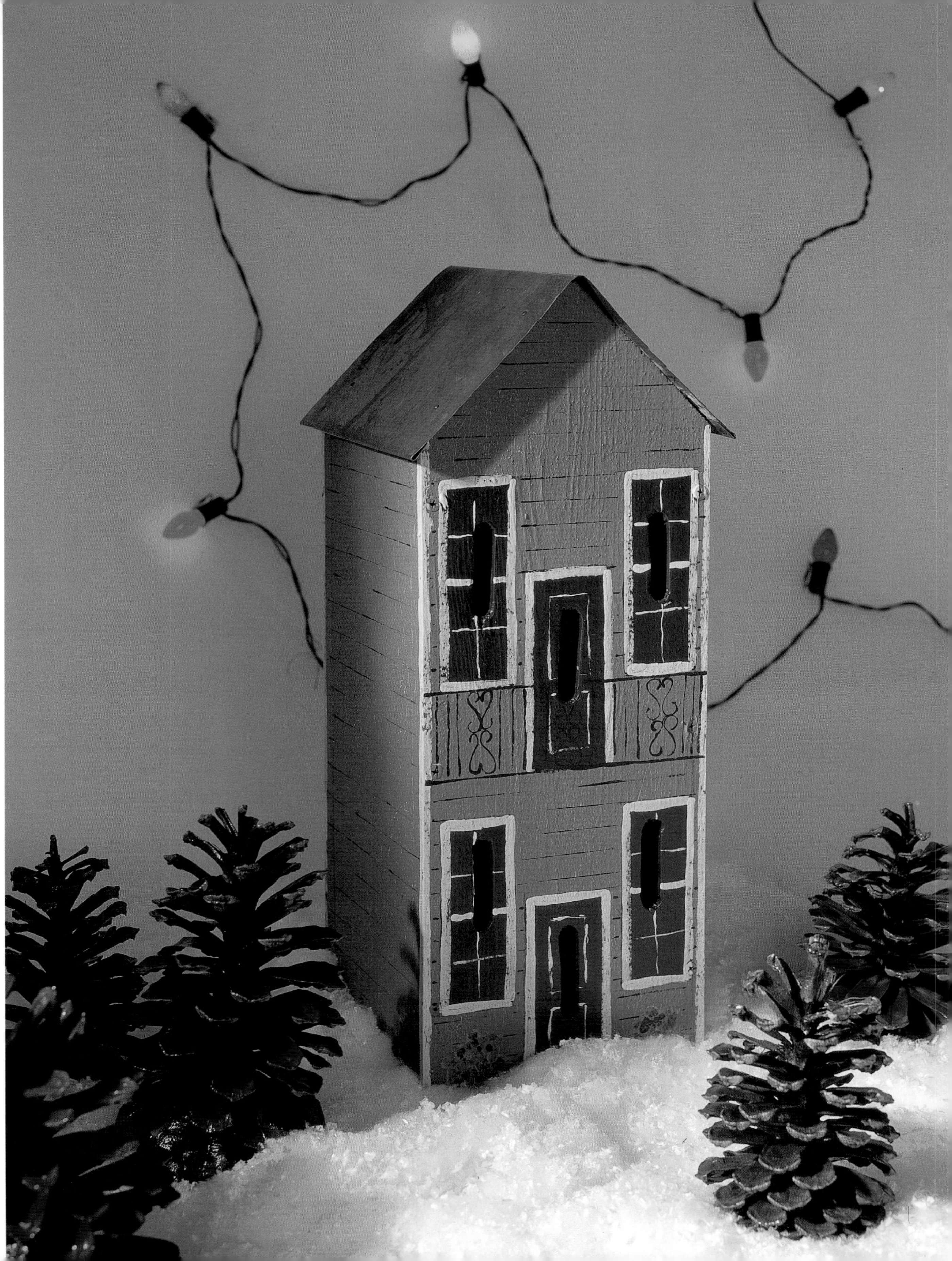

utterfly House

PROVIDING *shelter from sun and rain and a safe haven at night, this house adds color and charm to a garden. It should be placed in full or partial shade near flowering plants and shrubs.*

Materials

- pine or other commercial wood
- (2) 1 x 8 x 20-inch boards
- (2) 1 x 6 x 16-inch boards
- 1 x 6 x 6-inch boards
- 8½ x 13-inch copper or other sheet metal
- 1½-inch screws
- wood glue
- small wood nails
- acrylic paints or stains
- polyurethane

Tools

- table or hand saw
- router or ½-inch drill bit
- sabre saw
- screwdriver or power driver
- hammer
- paint brushes

Instructions

1. Make 45-degree cuts on the two 20-inch 1 x 8-inch boards for the roofline.

2. Cut six ½ x 2½-inch slots on one of these boards using a router or drill to open the hole, and a sabre saw to extend the slot. See the photo for general placement.

3. Assemble the box with glue and countersunk 1½-inch screws, sandwiching the two 16-inch boards between the 20-inch boards.

4. Prune and insert a branch to fit inside the chamber for the butterflies to light upon when inside.

5. Fit the 6 x 6-inch board into the bottom of the box flush, and attach with 1½-inch screws.

6. Fold the metal sheet in half and nail it to the top. (Both lids from a #10 can will suffice in lieu of sheet metal.)

7. Paint the house as you like. It could be stained and/or sealed with polyurethane, or left totally natural if the wood is cedar.

Garden Bench

HERE'S *a year-round gift idea that's relatively simple to make, but makes quite an impression sitting under the tree on Christmas morning.*

Materials

- white spruce, fir or pine
- for seat frame and slats
- (5) 1 x 4 x 40-inch boards
- (2) 2 x 4 x 40-inch boards
- (3) 2 x 4 x 15-inch boards

for front legs
- (2) 2 x 4 x 22½-inch boards

for rear legs and back
- (2) 2 x 6 x 36-inch boards

for armrests
- (2) 2 x 4 x 20-inch boards

for back slats
- 1 x 4 x 43-inch board
- 1 x 8 x 43-inch board
- 1½-inch wood screws
- 2½-inch wood screws
- wood glue

Tools

- table saw
- band, scroll or sabre saw
- screwdriver

Instructions

1. Assemble the seat frame using the three 15-inch 2 x 4's positioned at ends and center between, and perpendicular to, the two 40-inch 2 x 4's. Fasten with 2½-inch screws. (All the joints in this project are glued, and screws are countersunk.)

2. Attach the five 40-inch 1x4 slats to the frame with 1½-inch screws. The front slat extends one inch beyond the frame while the back slat is flush.

3. Attach the front legs to the seat with 2½-inch screws. The top surface of the seat is 17½-inch from the bottom of the leg.

4. The 2 x 6's used for the rear legs need to be angle cut for the contour. Use the band, scroll or sabre saw for the curves. Notch the upper back of the legs to receive the back slats, leaving a five-inch space between them. Attach these legs in the same fashion as the front ones.

5. Notch the armrests to match the contour of the back legs. They should extend one inch beyond the front legs. Round the corners as shown. Attach with 2½" screws.

6. To cut the contour on the upper back slat, draw a template for half the edge, trace it and flop it and trace the other half. Attach with 1½-inch screws.

7. Paint, stain or finish it as you like. To achieve this crackle finish, follow the directions in the Fish Carving project on pages 43–44.

Embellished Frames

THIS project proves how easy it can be to embellish any storebought frame, to create a one-of-a-kind gift for someone special—even more personal when you supply the picture.

Materials

- ◆ purchased frame
- ◆ silk or dried flowers
- ◆ organza ribbon
- ◆ small pinecones
- ◆ spanish moss
- ◆ brisa major
- ◆ small twigs

Tools

- ◆ scissors
- ◆ hot glue gun

Instructions

1. Arrange and cut the materials as you wish before you begin attaching them.

2. Use hot glue to attach the materials, starting with the larger objects, then filling in with the smaller ones.

3. The ribbons are added last, to complete the effect.

Scrap Frames

WITH *simple woodworking skills and an eye for found materials, you can easily create very "artsy" picture frames.*

Materials
- salvage frames
- wood scraps of trim pieces
- wooden dowels
- marbles
- other found objects
- acrylic paints
- nails and glues

Tools
- hand saw
- hammer
- paint brushes

Instructions

1. The raw frames can be found in many places: garage sales, thrift stores, flea markets, etc. Wider frames have more potential for embellishment.

2. Choose a design and a color scheme. Cut and arrange your decorative materials. Various painting techniques can be utilized at different stages of assembly, or all at once after assembly.

3. The components can be attached with nails and/or glue. Let dry.

4. Apply any paints or finishing treatments after construction.

**Christmas Crafts
Year-Round**

Jewelry

7

ONE *of the most personal gifts you can give to a loved one is jewelry. Consider the styles and colors of these baubles, bangles, and beads, and see how many ways you might create something very special for someone on your gift list.*

Painted Pins

Materials

- heavy weight watercolor paper
- assorted water base paints
- metallic paints or markers
- pin backs
- white glue or hot glue
- glossy acrylic varnish
- polymer resin (optional)

Tools

- paint brushes
- scissors
- pencil

Instructions

1. Sketch the outline of your design onto the paper, then cut or tear it out.

2. Paint it as you wish, and let dry.

3. Further decorations can include the use of beads, sequins, glitter glue, fabric paints, etc.

4. Brush on acrylic varnish to the design side of the paper, and let dry.

5. The optional polymer resin can be applied at this stage, following manufacturer's instructions, for greater strength and durability.

6. Varnish the back surface, and let dry.

7. Glue on the pin back.

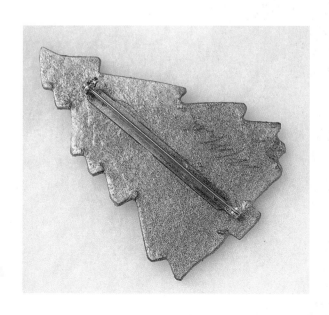

Charm Necklace

Materials

- ◆ perforated charms
- ◆ complementary beads
- ◆ beading thread or fishing line

Tools

- ◆ scissors

Instructions

1. Gather up your charm pieces—the older and more sentimental, the better.

2. Go to a bead store and find whatever elements will tie your piece together, in terms of color and shape.

3. You can see this design, for inspiration, but you will find your own.

4. When you finish, tie the ends together and feed them back into the adjoining beads to hide them.

Paper Earrings

Materials

- heavy weight water color paper
- assorted water base paints
- metallic inks and markers
- clear or other nail polishes
- craft glue
- sequins, beads, etc.
- earring post backs
- clear spray acrylic sealer

Tools

- scissors
- small paint brushes

Instructions

1. Cut free-form shapes out of the heavy paper.

2. Plan your design and color scheme, and gather your materials.

3. Apply your paints and inks, and let dry.

4. Nail polish can now be drizzled over the design, and sequins and beads sprinkled over top to dry.

5. Attach earring post backs with craft glue, and let dry.

6. Spray the entire surface with acrylic sealer.

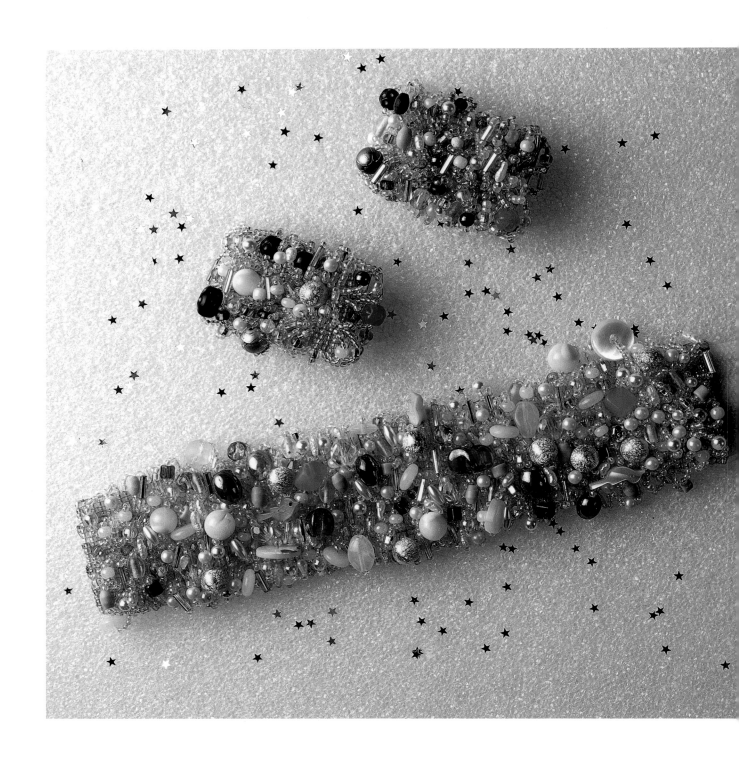

Beaded Bracelet and Earrrings

Materials

- assorted beads
- thread
- craft glue
- thin cardboard
- scrap of fabric or decorative paper
- earring post backs
- small strip of hook-and-loop tape

Tools

- bead loom
- beading needle
- scissors

Instructions

1. The base for both earrings and bracelet is prepared on a loom (see Pet Collars project, page 100). Secure the thread by entering one row, then the next, creating a circle.

2. String on rows of beads, with spacing like four plain, one special, four plain. Enter the base in one row, exit through another, securing the thread.

3. Continue stringing on beads as you like, then loop the thread back into the base. Continue until you have the density of beads you desire.

4. Secure the thread by making a circle: right to left on one row, left to right on the next row, and right to left on the original row.

5. To finish the earrings, pull the strings out of sight and glue the base to small panels of thin cardboard. Fabric or paper can be glued to the back for a more finished look. Glue the post backs to this.

6. To finish the bracelet, cut a pair of hook-and-loop strips to fit the width, with the rough piece being a little longer. Pull the strings back and glue the soft strip flush with the edge of the bracelet.

7. On the other end of the bracelet, but on the same surface, glue the rough strip to the end so that it hangs over about half the width of the soft strip. This allows both strips to overlap and lay flatter than if you glued the rough piece to the opposite surface.

8. When the glue is dry, cut away strings and clean up any glue spills.

Garnet Glass Necklace and Bracelet

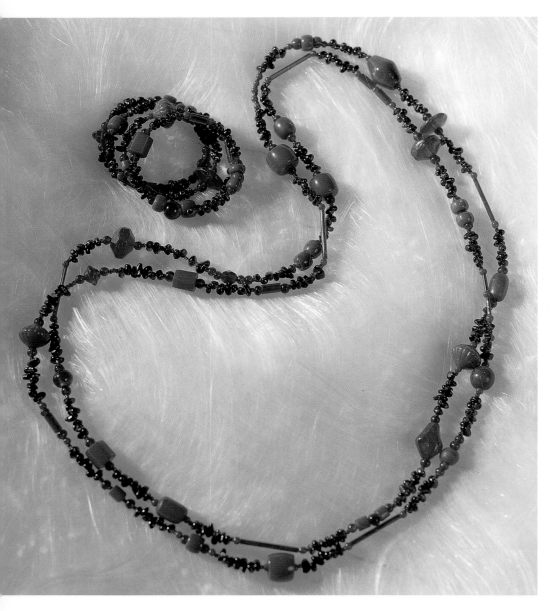

Necklace

Materials

- 75 inches (1.9 m) .019-inch diameter soft-flex wire or tiger tail wire

- 6 crimp beads

- 36-inch (91.4 cm) strand garnet chips

- 8 grams silver lined red seed beads, size 10 or 11

- 8 grams silver lined red bugle beads, size ½ inch–1 inch (1.3–2.5 cm)

- 24 assorted red glass beads, ½ inch (1.3 cm) or larger

- 5-6 dozen assorted red glass beads, ¼ inch –½ inch (.6–1.3 cm)

Tools

- needle nose pliers

- masking tape

- scissors

- egg carton, or other holder for beads

Instructions

1. Wrap masking tape around one end of the 75 inches (1.9 m) wire, about 3 inches (7.6 cm) from the end.

2. Begin threading beads onto the wire: seven garnet chips, seed bead, grouping of glass beads, seed bead, seven garnet chips, seed bead, grouping of glass beads, etc. Try to keep the glass bead grouping roughly the same length as the seed bead grouping. If some glass groups are longer, try to space the long groupings between two short ones.

SHORT   LONG   SHORT

3. When you are about 3 to 4 inches (7 to 10 cm) from the end of the wire, finish with a glass bead grouping, then string seed bead, garnet chip, crimp bead, garnet chip, crimp bead... ending with a garnet chip.

4. Carefully remove the tape from the beginning end of the wire, and put that end through the garnet/crimp grouping just completed. Gently pull both ends so that any spaces between beads is eliminated.

5. When beads are snug but not taut, gently smash crimps closed with the needle nose pliers. Trim the ends with scissors, getting as close to the garnets as possible.

Bracelet

Materials

- 22 inches (60 cm) or four complete loops of bright memory wire
- 15-inch (38 cm) strand garnet chips
- 36-inch (91.4 cm) strand silver lined red glass seed beads, size 10 or 11
- 6 assorted red glass beads, ½ inch (1.3 cm) or larger
- 4 dozen assorted red glass beads, ¼ inch–½ inch (.6–1.3 cm)

Tools

- needle nose pliers
- wire cutters
- egg carton, or other holder for beads

Instructions

1. Make a tiny loop with the pliers in one end of the memory wire. The wire is very stiff, so apply yourself.

2. Begin threading beads onto the wire: seed bead, seven garnet chips, seed bead, glass bead grouping, seed bead, seven garnet chips, seed bead, etc. Try to keep the glass bead grouping about as long as the garnet grouping.

3. When the wire is filled up to the last ¼ inch, gently push the beads together to close up any gaps. Then, with the pliers, carefully bend the end of the wire into another tiny loop. Hold the beads gently, but twist the wire hard, and be patient.

Unakite Necklace and Earrings

Materials

- size A silamide or size D nymo thread (waxed)
- 8 grams #11 salmon pearl seed beads (coded A)
- 8 grams #11 prussian blue pearl seed beads (coded B)
- 8 grams #11 any S.L. moss green seed beads (coded C)
- (2) 8mm coral glass beads
- (4) 6mm pale green glass beads
- (4) gold bead caps
- (2) 1-inch x ¾-inch (2.5 x 1.9 cm) double-drilled unakite stone beads
- two gold bead tips
- two side-cut or oval jump rings
- your choice of clasp

Tools

- #6 twist wire or size 10 steel needles
- scissors

Necklace

Instructions

1. This is a free-form necklace where the spaces between strands create focal points. Tie four 1-yard strands of thread together with an overhand knot, then go through the bead tip and begin: 2C, 4A, 2C, 4B, 2C, 4A, 4C. Repeat for 8½ inches (21.6 cm).

2. Bring four strands together through a 6mm green glass bead. Separate into single strands and add 3A each, then four strands together through an 8mm coral bead with bead caps on either side. Separate back into single strands and add 3B each.

3. Bring four strands together through another 6mm green bead, then separate back into four strands and add to each: 4C, 4A, 2C, 4B, 4A, 4C.

4. Bring two strands through the top hole of a unakite stone, and two strands through the bottom. On the other side, take two bottom strands through the top hole of a second unakite stone and two top strands through the bottom, forming an "X" in the following pattern: 4A, 2C, 4B, 2C, 4A, 2C, 4B, 2C, 4A, 2C, 4B, 2C, 4A...

5. Complete the second side in reverse.

6. After attaching the clasp, tie two loose overhead knots in the strands on either side as you wish.

Earrings

Added Materials

- gold drop or earwire loop
- jeweler's glue

Instructions

1. Begin by making two spacers with five columns of: 1A, 1B, 1A... (Follow same instructions for spacers as in Four-Strand Necklace and Earrings project, page 92.)

2. Leave a 4-inch tail and go up through the first column. Add: 2A, 2C, 2B, 1A, 6C, 1A, 2B, 2C, 2A... down through the last column, and weave five dangles: 3C, 1B, 1A, 1B, 1C, 2B, 1A, 2B, 3C, 1A, 1B, 1A.

3. Tie off with the beginning thread, glue and clip.

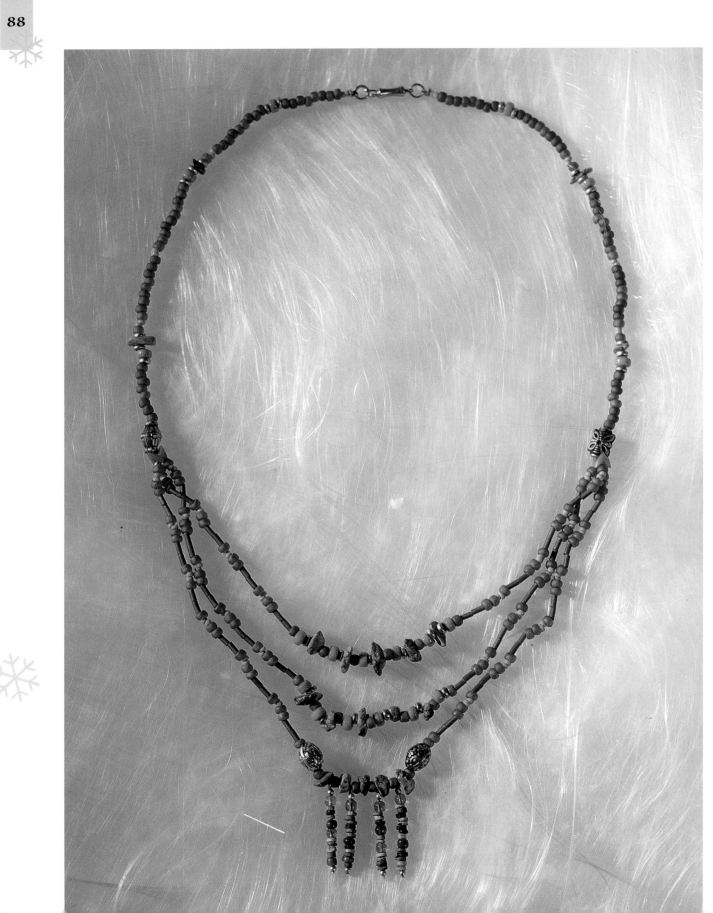

Three-Strand Necklace

Materials

- FF nylon or #6 no-stretch beadstring
- jeweler's glue
- your choice of clasp
- 2 jumprings
- 2 bead tips
- size 6 japanese matte seed beads in three colors (your choice)
- one pack japanese matte bugle beads (your choice)
- 4 grams turquoise chips
- 4 silver 10mm beads
- 18 orange african glass rondelles
- 36 brass rondelles
- 4 headpins
- small assortment of 4mm glass beads for dangles

Tools

- #6 twisted wire needles
- scissors

Instructions

1. Make four dangles first by stringing 1 inch of 4mm beads on headpins, and making a loop at the top. These will be added last.

2. Cut three 56-inch (142 cm) lengths of thread, each of which will be doubled. Tie all strands together with an overhead knot. Go through the bead tip and string 6½ inches (16.5 cm) of variously colored matte beads with turquoise chips, african glass, and brass rondelles at equal intervals.

3. Go through a silver bead and separate into three strands. You are now in the center section.

4. The top strand will be 8 inches (20.3 cm), the middle strand 9 inches (22.9 cm), and the bottom strand 10 inches (25.4 cm). The two silver beads in the bottom strand are separated by 1½ inches (3.8 cm), between which the four dangles are attached. Center sections in the other two strands are 2 inches (5.1 cm) long, and contain turquoise chips, brass rondelles and african glass.

5. Repeat other side in reverse, go through a bead tip, knot and glue.

6. Attach clasp to bead tips with jump rings.

Peyote Stitch Necklace and Bracelet

Materials
- soft macrame cord
- beading thread
- lots of beads, your choice of colors

Tools
- beading needle
- scissors

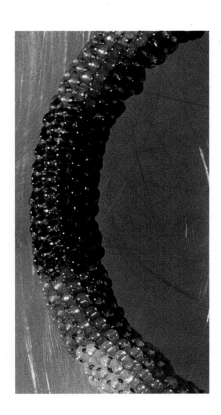

Instructions

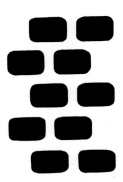

1. Cut your macrame cord a few inches longer than your intended length. Thread a needle with a long length of thread, stitch it to the cord, and begin threading enough beads to circle the cord. Once you have done this, anchor the strand through the first bead, then proceed around each turn, anchoring as you go.

2. As you come to the end of your thread, wrap the beaded length around the cord and stitch it down. Then stitch on a new length and continue until you have covered the cord.

3. When the beadwork is completed, cut away the excess cord, being careful not to cut away any structural threads. Sew the cord together, and fill in any space with beads as before.

4. Any dangles can be added individually by sewing directly into the cord, through the beaded strands.

5. The bracelet is constructed in the same manner, with some extra bead tailings to cover the seam.

Four-Strand Necklace and Earrings

Materials

- size A silamide or size D nymo thread (waxed)
- 16 grams #11 amethyst seed beads (coded A)
- 16 grams ¼-inch (.6 cm) black bugle beads (coded B)
- 22 6mm faceted black glass beads
- 4 top-drilled black tubular or teardrop beads
- jeweler's glue

Tools

- #6 twist wire or size 10 steel needles
- scissors

Necklace

Instructions

1. To make four bugle bead spacers, cut two feet (61 cm) of thread, string on two bugles positioned in the middle of the thread. Go back through the first bugle, then back through the second. Pull thread so both beads are together vertically. Add third bugle, go back through second , back through third, then add three more bugles using same procedure. Tie off with a square knot, glue, let dry, and clip excess thread.

2. Pattern for center of necklace #1: 10A, 1B, 1A, 1B repeated six times.

3. Then add 2A, bugle spacer, and Pattern #2: 2A, 1B, 1A, 1B, 10A, 1B, 1A, 1B, 10A.

4. Add a 6mm bead, repeat Pattern #2, then add a bugle spacer. Repeat Pattern #2, then add a 6mm bead, 5A, a top-drilled tubular, 5A, a 6mm, 5A, a top-drilled, 5A, then a 6mm.

5. Continue this pattern to complete the other side of the center of the necklace.

6. Next cut two 2-yard (1.8 m) lengths of thread and thread them both on a twist needle. Put on 26 A beads and push them to the center of the thread. This will be the loop fastener.

7. Bring all four ends of thread through the needle, and go through 6 A beads. Take the needle off. You'll now have four separate threads. Work on all four con-currently using four needles to avoid miscounting.

8. When you've completed side two, bring all four strands together again through 6 A beads and then a 6mm. Add about 9 A beads until you've covered the 6mm bead. Come out the bottom of the 6mm, remove needle, take two threads in each hand and tie two square knots on top of each other. Glue, dry and clip.

9. The 18 dangles will be spaced evenly between the three center 6mm beads. Two dangles have top-drilled beads, all the others 6mm. The pattern for the top-drilled: 4A, 1B, 6A, 1B, 6A, 6mm, 3A, 3A and back through these three go back up through dangle, through 2A in main body of neclace and begin next dangle.

10. The pattern for 6mm dangles: 4A, 1B, 6A, 1B, 6A, 6mm, 3A, 3A and back through and up dangle again. Tie, glue, dry and clip all dangles.

Earrings

Added Materials

- (2) 6mm faceted black glass beads
- (4) 4mm czech glass crystal beads
- 2 square black buttons
- 1 pair niobium french wires

Instructions

1. Using the same technique for making bugle spacers, substitute 2 A beads for each bugle. Begin at back hole of button, leaving a 6-inch (15.2 cm) tail of thread, and weave around button tightly until you return to back hole, go through, tie off at begin-ning tail, glue, dry and clip.

2. To make top loop, pick up 10 A beads on thread, which will run under-neath the top of the band of beads again to form loop. Tie off, glue, dry and clip.

3. For the bottom loop, take thread under main band, pick up 7 A beads, 1 crys-tal, 6A, a 6mm, 6A, 1 crystal, 7A. Go through loop one more time for strength, tie, glue, dry and clip. Attach ear wires to top loop.

Necklace with Ceramic Crescent

Materials

- ◆ ceramic crescent with holes
- ◆ assorted seed beads
- ◆ assorted glass beads
- ◆ waxed beading thread
- ◆ jeweler's glue

Tools

- ◆ beading needle
- ◆ scissors

Instructions

1. This is a free-form design that lends itself to found objects and leftover beads. The crescent could be found or made yourself, and needn't even be ceramic, but should have holes in the approximate positions shown. Consider shells, twigs, driftwood, bones, rocks, metal or other shards in place of the crescent used here. Like elements can be used in place of the glass beads as well.

2. The double strand shown here is entwined, tied into a jumble toward the ends, then tied through a bead and into the corner holes of the crescent. Secure with glue, let dry and clip the excess threads.

3. The dangles are doubled and secured at their bottoms and behind the crescent by knotting the threads around seed beads.

Lariat Necklace

Materials

- no-stretch nylon bead thread or size A silamide thread
- 4 packs assorted seed beads
- 1 pack bugle beads or 2 oz. liquid silver bugles
- 2 headpins
- your choice of focal beads

Tools

- size 10 steel needles
- jeweler's glue
- scissors

Instructions

1. Not even a clasp to worry about, just wrap and sling—an easy beginner's project. Make a loop of 28 seed beads with a 4-inch (10.2 cm) tail. Go back through at least once to reinforce, then thread on 21 inches (53.3 cm) of beads in a randomn pattern.

2. Go through a teardrop bead, add 16 seed beads, go back up through the teardrop, and back through the entire necklace to the beginning tail. Tie off, glue, dry and clip.

3. To the loop from the teardrop, attach with a headpin a vintage bead, or an old earring that's missing its mate.

4. To the beginning loop, attach five dangles of varying length.

5. To wear, pull the teardrop end through the beginning loop several times. Play with it.

Dreamcatcher Pin

Materials

- 2-inch (5 cm) safety pin with 3 loops
- 3 dreamcatcher earring hoops: 1-inch, ¾-inch, ½-inch (2.5, 1.9, 1.3 cm)
- 23 earth color stone chips
- 3 small peahen feathers
- (3) 4mm brass beads
- 1 skein brown cotton embroidery thread
- 3 small jump rings
- jeweler's glue

Tools

- #6 twisted wire needles
- scissors

Instructions

1. Using about 16 inches (40.6 cm) of thread, tie each hoop into a bottom loop of the pin with a slip knot. Glue, let dry and clip excess thread.

2. To weave the webs, begin with thread going underneath hoop, then over around and back through the loop, forming a half hitch knot. Add a stone chip and go back through it, then back to first step of under, over and through. These hoops have little notches for you to position each hitch.

3. Continue around the hoop to the beginning loop. In the second row around, you'll make your hitch around the thread after each chip, which will work just like the outside hoop. You'll go around a third time on each hoop, leaving a middle hole for the dreams to enter. Tie off, glue, dry and clip.

4. Glue feather stems into brass beads and clip the feather tops. When dry, leave a 2-inch (5 cm) tail on thread run up through feather, around hoop and back down through feather. Tie, glue, dry and clip.

Beaded Scarf

Materials

- ◆ purchased scarf
- ◆ assorted beads
- ◆ thread

Tools

- ◆ beading needle
- ◆ scissors

Instructions

1. Find beads to complement whatever scarf you choose to embellish.

2. The foundation strip for the dangles shown here was a loomed beadwork piece as described in the preceding project. You can also use a strip of shiny fabric as a foundation, or sew dangles directly to the scarf.

3. Thread a needle and tie the end to one edge of the scarf. Add all the beads for one dangle, go around the last bead and back up through the dangle, pull taut and anchor back into the scarf before proceeding on to the next dangle. Tie off and clip.

*B*utton *Covers*

Materials

- ◆ ⅝-inch (1.6 cm) metal button covers
- ◆ oven-bake polymer clay
- ◆ acrylic paint
- ◆ spray sealer

Tools

- ◆ sculpting or manicure tools
- ◆ paint brushes

Instructions

1. Form and shape the clay over the button cover. For quilt squares, indent the border and pattern the surface with a flat-edge sculpting tool. Use the same technique for pumpkin ridges, subsequently adding leaf and stem. The flowers are fashioned by adding one petal at a time. For the snowman, first shape the body, then arms, hat scarf, and wreath.

2. Bake them in the oven following manufacturer's directions, and let cool.

3. Rather than using the colored clays and painting over certain parts, which yields a plastic appearance, use a neutral clay and paint over the entire surface with a fine brush. Let dry.

4. Spray on the sealer.

Note: This sort of button can be worn severally on jackets and sweaters, but also as the single top button for a brooch effect.

Pet Collars

Materials

- purchased pet collars
- assorted seed beads
- size 0 beading thread
- craft glue

Tools

- a beading loom
- beading needles
- scissors

Instructions

1. You can easily make your own loom with a raw stretcher frame or cheap picture frame. Position small push pins or nails in two rows across from each other.

2. Plan your bead design on graph paper, creating a grid of each bead's color.

3. Tie thread to a corner pin, then loop it back and forth across opposite pins until you have one more thread than the number of bead rows in your design's width. It should be taut before you tie it off.

4. Cut a thread about 18 inches (45.7 cm). Tie one end to the bottom left warp thread about 3–4 inches (7.6–10.2 cm) from the frame. Thread the other end through a needle.

5. Following your graphed design from left to right, string the first row of beads onto the needle and thread. Push the beads to the tied end, then pull them up against the warp so the fit between those threads. Now come around over top with the needle and go back through the beads right to left, using finger pressure from underneath the beads so the needle can find its way.

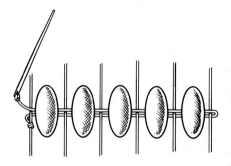

6. Continue each row in this manner until your design is completed. Circle through your last row once again to secure it before tying it off. If you run out of thread before your design is complete, finish it in the same way. Then circle the new thread through the previous row before continuing on.

7. Cut warp threads from loom as close to frame as possible. Tie these end threads in pairs with square knots to secure both ends. Clip excess to an inch or so.

8. Tuck these threads underneath the piece when you glue it to the collar, and let dry. You may want to reinforce the ends with a few stitches into the collar.

Christmas Crafts
Year-Round

Sewing and
Crochet

BECAUSE

*herbs have special
healing properties, you
can create these little pillows and sachets that have more
to offer than just ornamental value. They are fairly easy to
make, and can be tailor-made for anyone on your gift list.*

Herb
Pillows

Calming Pillow for Baby *(top)*

Materials

- 1 pair Battenburg or crochet doilies
- small white cotton lining fabric
- 1⅓ yards (1.22 m) satin ribbon
- 1–1½ cups dill weed

Tools

- sewing machine
- basic sewing tools
- funnel

Instructions

1. Press the doilies using spray sizing to stiffen them slightly, adjusting them to align as you iron.

2. Cut two thicknesses of lining to fit the center portion of the doilies, adding ½" (1.3 cm) margin for seam allowance all around. This will form the herb-filled sack.

3. Layer the pieces in this manner:

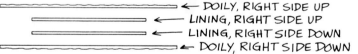

← DOILY, RIGHT SIDE UP
← LINING, RIGHT SIDE UP
← LINING, RIGHT SIDE DOWN
← DOILY, RIGHT SIDE DOWN

4. Stitch through all thicknesses, following the interior lace pattern of the shape you've chosen, ½" (1.3 cm) in from the outer edge of the lining fabric, leaving a ½"–1" (1.3–2.5 cm) opening on one side.

5. Fill the lining with dill, using a funnel. Stitch the opening closed.

6. Trim the raw edges of lining with pinking shears close to the seam.

7. Tie and tack on bows for trim.

Note: The word "dill" is derived from the Latin "to lull". It has been brewed in households over an open fire for centuries to pacify fussy babies. This pillow can be placed in a crib to help your baby, and you, have a peaceful night's sleep. (You may want to include this in your gift card.)

Dream Pillow *(lower right)*

Materials

- ¼ yard (30 cm) tapestry fabric
- ¼ yard (30 cm) chiffon or organza fabric
- 4 yards (3.66 m) very thin cording
- 1 decorative frog or other closure
- 3 cups herbal dream blend

Tools

- sewing machine
- basic sewing tools
- large-eyed needle

Instructions

1. Blend the following herbs: lavender, rose petals, hops, rosemary, mints, chamomile, cedar tips, mugwort, cloves, etc. ...or any blend that pleases you.

2. Cut a 7" x 13" (17.8 x 33 cm) rectangle from the tapestry fabric, and again for the chiffon. Place right sides together, and trim the pieces as illustrated:

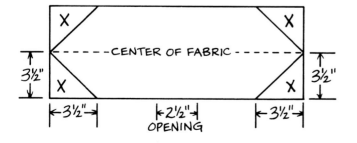

3. With right sides together, stitch all sides with a ½" (1.3 cm) seam allowance, leaving a 2½" (6.4 cm) opening on one side. Turn inside out and press.

4. Topstitch ¼" (.6 cm) from edge around all sides, leaving same opening. Also stitch a perpendicular seam through both thicknesses 3" (7.6 cm) from the point on each end. This creates the pocket for the herbs.

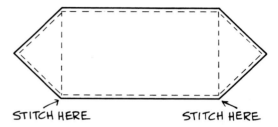

5. Fill the cavity with herbs, then top-stitch it closed.

6. Trim these edges with cording using an overcast stitch. Use the top stitch as a guide. Be careful to hide the knots. Fold the two points inward 'til they touch.

7. Position the frog closure, and tack it in place.

Note: Dream pillows have been used throughout history to promote deep, restful sleep. Romans used rose petals, Victorians dispelled melancholy with lavender, while rosemary is reputed to prevent nightmares, cloves to prevent snoring. Hops, mugwort, chamomile, and mint are all sedatives. (You may want to include this in your gift card.)

Lavender Eye Pillow *(left)*

Materials

- ⅙ yard (15.2 cm) chiffon or organza
- ⅙ yard (15.2 cm) satin fabric
- ⅓ yard (30.5 cm) 2" (5.1 cm) wide lace
- 4 yards (3.66 m) ⅛" or ¹⁄₁₆" (.3 or .15 cm) double faced satin ribbon
- 1½ cups flax seed
- 1 cup lavender flowers
- 10 drops essential oil of lavender

Tools

- sewing machine
- basic sewing tools
- large-eye needle for ribbon
- funnel
- mixing bowl
- plastic bag

Instructions

1. Mix flax seed, lavender and oil in a bowl, transfer to a plastic bag, and let them meld for 24 hours.

2. Cut one 5" x 11" (12.7 x 28 cm) panel out of the satin, two 5" x 11" panels out of the chiffon, and the lace to 11" (28 cm).

3. Layer the pieces in this manner:

SATIN, RIGHT SIDE DOWN
CHIFFON, RIGHT SIDE UP
LACE, RIGHT SIDE UP
CHIFFON, RIGHT SIDE UP

4. Stitch through all thicknesses with a ½" (1.3 cm) seam allowance, leaving a 1½" (3.8 cm) opening on one side.

5. Turn inside out, and press. Top-stitch about ³⁄₁₆" (.45 cm) in from each side of the opening.

6. Fill with lavender mix using funnel, then top-stitch the opening closed.

7. Trim with ribbon using an overcast stitch, with the top-stitch line as a guide. Hide knots on the back side.

Note: Flax seed provides gentle influence over the eye muscles, and lavender relaxes, so that this pillow is a great stress reliever. Lay on your back, place the pillow over your eyes, and breathe deeply. This works for mid-day naps, and just before bed time.

Comfort Sack *(lower right)*

Materials

- ⅓ yard (30.5 cm) tapestry or other outside fabric
- ⅓ yard (30.5 cm) lining fabric
- 5 cups small dry bean
- (10) 3-inch (7.6 cm) sticks cinnamon, broken
- ¼ cup whole cloves
- 1⅔ yards (1.52 m) cording

Tools

- sewing machine
- basic sewing tools

Instructions

1. From the tapestry, cut: one 9" x 17½" (23 x 44.5 cm) panel, and two 9" x 12" (23 x 30.5 cm) panels. From the lining, cut: two 9" x 17½" (23 x 44.5 cm) panels.

2. With right sides of lining facing, stitch ½" (1.3 cm) from outer edge all the way around, except for a 3" (7.6 cm) opening on one of the long sides. Turn right side out and press.

3. Fill lining with beans, cloves, and cinnamon, then stitch the opening closed.

4. On a 9" x 12" (23 x 30.5 cm) piece of tapestry, press under ½" (1.3 cm) on one 9" (23 cm) edge, then fold over again and press. Stitch ¼" (.6 cm) from edge through all thicknesses, then repeat for the second 9" x 12" (23 x 30.5 cm) piece.

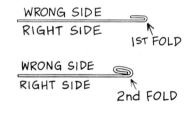

5. Layer the tapestry pieces as shown at right.

6. Stitch through all thicknesses, with a ½" (1.3 cm) seam allowance all around. Turn and press. Insert lining sack with the bean and spice mix.

7. Fold excess fabric under sack, then tie with cording.

Note: (Include this information in your gift card:) Remove the cording and place the entire sack in a microwave oven for 3–7 minutes on high. Use as you would a heating pad, and enjoy the pleasant aroma as well as almost 45 minutes of heat.

Envelope Pillows

HERE'S *a great way to dress up an old, faded pillow, or to quickly adapt to changing color schemes in new furnishings.*

Materials

- a square pillow
- heavy fabric remnant
- fringe or other trim
- decorative buttons (optional)
- thread

Tools

- sewing machine
- basic sewing tools

Instructions

1. Cut fabric 3 inches (7.6 cm) longer than the pillow by 3.5 times the pillow. For instance, if your pillow is 16 inches (40.6 cm) square, your fabric should be cut 19" x 56" (48.3 x 142 cm).

2. Stitch a 2" (5.1 cm) hem on both of the short sides of the rectangular fabric.

3. Place the fabric, back side down, with the short ends at the top and bottom. Fold the bottom up approximately 12" (30.5 cm) from the top. Pin in place.

4. Fold top of fabric down so it overlaps 2 inches (5.1 cm) of the fold made by the bottom.

5. Stitch the laft and right long sides approximately ½" (1.3 cm) from the edge.

6. Turn right side out. Add any trim or buttons you like.

7. Insert pillow.

Tapestry Tote

THIS *is a sturdy bag that can be used for many purposes, from knitting supplies to shopping excursions.*

Materials

- ⅔ yard (61 cm) tapestry fabric
- ⅔ yard (61 cm) lining fabric
- 1½ yards (46 cm) 2" (5 cm) wide nylon webbing or seat belt strap
- 1 yard (91 cm) cording
- large decorative button

Tools

- sewing machine
- basic sewing tools

Instructions

1. Cut from the tapestry: two 19" (48.3 cm) squares, two 27" x 2¾" (68.6 x 7 cm) strips, and one 10" x 5" (25.4 x 12.7 cm) panel. Cut from lining: two 19" (48.3 cm) squares, and one 10" x 5" (25.4 x 12.7 cm) panel.

2. Fold under ½" (1.3 cm) and press on both long sides of the 27" (68.6 cm) strips of tapestry, making their width 1¾" (4.4 cm). Center the tapestry on the strapping, right side up, and stitch along both sides, ⅛" (.3 cm) from the edges. These will be the handles.

3. Right sides together, using ½" (1.3 cm) seam allowance, stitch the two sides and the bottom of the 19" (48.3 cm) tapestry squares. Repeat for the lining squares. Turn each and press the seams open. Then press down ½" (1.3 cm) along the upper edge of each.

4. For the flap closure, first cut a 20"
   (50.8 cm) length of cording, fold it in half,
   knot it 1" (2.5 cm) from that fold, then
   again 1¼" (3.2 cm) from that knot.

5. Trim the 10" x 5" (25.4 x 12.7 cm) tapestry
   and lining panels as shown below.

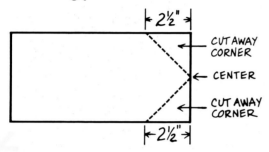

6. Layer the tapestry, lining, and cording as
   shown below. The tapestry should be right
   side down, and the lining right side up.
   The cord ends extend slightly beyond the
   diagonal edges of the fabric.

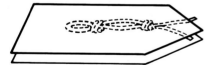

7. Stitch along all sides except the 5" (12.7 cm)
   side. Turn and press, then topstitch ¼"
   (.6 cm) from the edge on all sides.

8. Slip the lining bag inside the tapestry bag,
   with right sides out, and wrong sides facing
   in. Pin the upper edge together, inserting the
   handles on each side, and the flap on the
   back side ½" (1.3 cm) below the upper edge.
   Be sure the flap is centered and the handles
   line up. Topstitch all around the upper edge,
   ¼" (.6 cm) from folded over edges.

9. Using the flap and cording to find its position, sew the button firmly in place. For
   decoration, loop a 10" (25.4 cm) length of
   cording around the button and knot the ends.

Lace Trim Towels

CREATING *coordinated gift sets of towels like these is almost embarrasingly simple, but see how spectacular the results can be.*

Materials
- purchased towels
- lace trim and matching thread

Tools
- sewing needle or machine
- scissors

Instructions

1. Find lace that will launder well, with minimal shrinkage or puckering. This will reduce or even prevent the need for ironing.

2. Cut lace to the width of the towel, adding ¼" (.6 cm) to each end for turning under.

3. Fold the ¼" (.6 cm) under and stitch up the side, then across the top and down the other folded side. The bottom usually will not need to be stitched.

Covered Scrapbook

SCRAPBOOKS *can be used and enjoyed for many years by people of all ages. They become even greater keepsakes when they are handmade and personalized in this way.*

Materials

- 24 sheets 9" x 12" (or any stock size) heavyweight paper
- 2 pieces 9" x 12" museum board or heavy cardboard
- 2 pieces 9" x 12" cotton or linen fabric
- 2 pieces 13" x 16" (or 10 cm larger than paper) cotton or linen fabric
- 2 pieces 13" x 16" cotton lace
- 2 yards (1.8 m) ribbon
- fabric glue
- anti-fraying glue

Tools

- scissors
- heavy-duty hole punch
- craft knife

Instructions

1. After cutting out your fabric pieces, punch four holes, in matching positions, on one short edge of both pieces of heavy board. Lightly score a line with a knife across these holes on one side of each board. Punch holes in the paper to match these.

2. Turn under and press a ½" (1.3 cm) seam around every piece of fabric (not the lace).

3. Lay one of the large pieces of fabric face down. Lay one of the boards, scored line up, in the center of the fabric. Wrap and glue the fabric around each edge of the board, folding the corners. With small pointed scissors, open the fabric over the holes in the board, then apply anti-fraying glue to prevent unravelling. Repeat for other board.

4. Repeat this procedure for the lace, positioning the holes in the lace over the holes in the board. Then glue the smaller pieces of fabric over top as a liner.

5. Assemble the book and bind it with the ribbon.

Medieval Hats

THESE *make really fun gifts for any fashion adventurous people on your list. In fact, they're liable to bring out the eccentric in most of us.*

Materials

- 24" (61 cm) square of brocade
- 18" (46 cm) square of velvet
- 1" x 2" (2.5 x 5 cm) elastic band
- thread

Tools

- sewing machine
- basic sewing tools
- paper for patterns
- transparent tape

Instructions

1. To make your patterns, draw an equilateral triangle with each side 5½" (14 cm) long. Make four copies. Cut out the five triangles and tape them onto another sheet of paper, points touching, as shown at right.

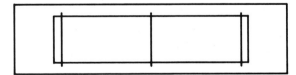

   Cut out the outline of this shape. On another sheet of paper, cut out a circle 7" (17.8 cm) in diameter.

2. If your brocade has a good selvage, you can use it on the hat band for a nice finishing touch, but it's not necessary. Cut a 24" x 4" (61 x 10.2 cm) strip (include selvage if desired) for the hat band. Place the star pattern on the remaining brocade and cut it out.

3. Take the brocade star and place it face down on the velvet so that both right sides are touching. Using the brocade as a pattern, cut out the velvet star. Then place the circle pattern in the center of the velvet star, pin it and cut it out.

4. Pin the stars together, right sides facing, and sew them together with a seam that is only ¼" (.6 cm). If you are not able to serge this seam, go back and zigzag the edges so they don't pull apart.

5. Sew the hat band ends together to form a circle. Pin this circle to the circular velvet opening, with the right side of the hat band facing the wrong side of the velvet. Ease the opening if necessary, or make the hat band smaller by making a deeper seam where it joins. Don't pin the selvage side.

6. Sew this to hat with a ¼"–½" (.6–1.3 cm) seam. Turn inside out (using a pencil to poke the star points out), and fold the hat band to the front.

7. Pin the band in place, either leaving selvage showing or folding the cut edge under. Sew the band down.

8. If you think the hat may be too loose and you want a snug fit, sew one edge of elastic at the back seam, then pull as far as it will stretch and pin it down. Sew. Pull elastic until it lays flat on the hat band and pin it in the middle. Sew.

   If head is larger than 23 inches (58.4 cm), make the circle ½" (1.3 cm) bigger. Also add 1 inch (2.5 cm) to head size for the hat band. This may affect the amount of brocade needed.

9. To make the triangular hat, follow the same directions except for the pattern. In place of the star, draw an equilateral triangle with 18" (45.7 cm) sides. Also, sew bells or beads to the points of the triangle.

Book Marker

*A **MOST** useable gift that requires only basic skills in crochet, and something you can make in your spare time year-round.*

Materials

♦ 50 yards (45.7 m) size D silk thread

Tools

♦ #8 steel crochet hook
♦ pins
♦ corrugated cardboard

Instructions

1. The pattern for the first row is: CH 20, in 8th CH from hook (2 DC, CH 2, 2 DC), CH 1, in 4th CH from last (1 DC), CH 1, in 4th CH from last (2 DC, CH 2, 2 DC), CH 1 in 4th CH from last 1 DC.

2. For the second row: CH 4, turn. (2 DC, CH 2, 2 DC), in 2 CH space between DC's, CH 1, 1 DC in top of DC, CH 1, (2 DC, CH 2, 2 DC), in 2 CH space between DC's, CH 1, 1 DC in top of CH 4.

3. Repeat until you reach desired length, making sure there are an odd number of rows.

4. For edging: CH 3 (turn work to the side, then edge down one side and up the other), DC, CH 2, 2 DC in CH 4 space. (CH 1, SC, CH 1) in next CH 4 space. (2 DC, CH 2, 2 DC) in next CH 4 space, (CH 1, 1 SC, CH 1) in next CH 4 space. Repeat up to corner.

5. In corner: (2 DC, 2 CH, 2DC), SC, (2 DC, 2 CH, 2 DC), CH 1, 1 SC in space, CH 1, (2 DC, CH 2, 2 DC) on top of DC, CH 1, 1 SC in space, CH 1. Corner like the last corner.

6. Repeat the pattern down the other side, ending with final DC. Cut thread.

7. Weave the end threads into stitches. Knot four tassels evenly across the bottom. Each tassel consists of 5- to 6-inch (13–15 cm) strands folded in half.

8. To block the piece: Draw a rectangle 1½" x 12" (3.8 x 30.5 cm) on cardboard. Soak the piece and wring out excess water. Stretch and pin the piece to the cardboard outline. Also pin at shell stitch points and down the sides. Let dry. You may even want to add spray starch before unpinning this piece.

Table Cloth

THIS *piece is so beautiful, it could even be used as a shawl. This should inspire you to utilize this technique for any number of purposes.*

Materials

- 12 yards (11 m) sewing thread in about four shades
- 28 strands x 7 inches (18 cm) long for fringe

Tools

- size 7 steel crochet hook

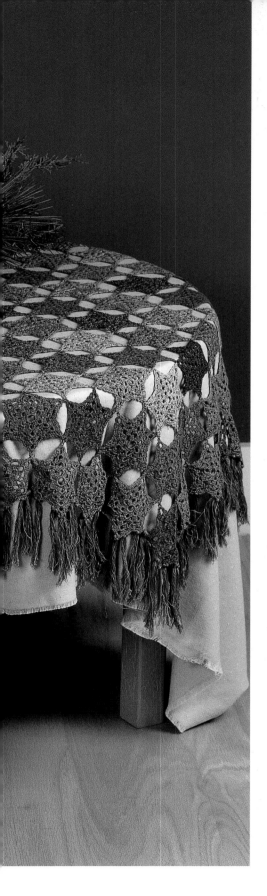

Instructions

1. The finished size of this table cloth is 52 inches (132 cm) in diameter, and contains 217 stars.

2. Initial directions are: CH 13, slip stitch (sl st) to join into the circle.

3. *Row 1:* CH 3 (always counts as first DC), 2 DC around chain, CH 5, 3 DC, CH 5 until there are six 3 DC groups. Join last CH 5 to top of beginning CH 3.

4. *Row 2:* sl st through tops of first 2 DC, CH 3, then 2 DC in CH loop, CH 5, 3 D, CH 1, in next CH loop 3 DC, 3 D, CH 1. Repeat in each CH loop. End with CH 1, sl st to top of beginning CH 3.

5. *Row 3:* sl st through tops of 2 DC. CH 3, 2 DC, CH 5, 3 DC in 5 CH loop, CH 3, 1 SC in CH 1 space, CH 3. 3 DC, CH 5, 3 DC, CH 3, 1 SC, CH 3. Repeat. End with sl st to top of original CH 3.

6. *Row 4:* sl st through tops of 2 DC. CH 3, 2 DC, CH 5, 3 DC in 5 CH loop, CH 3, DC in front of SC, DC in back of SC, CH 3. Repeat. End with sl st to first CH of original CH 3.

7. When joining these motifs together, the 5 CH loops meet so that when a point is coming up: CH 2, SC in the adjoining motif point, CH 2 equals 1, 5 CH loop. Two points of one motif join to two points of the next motif.

8. The final shape of the tablecloth is a hexagram. Begin at the center with one motif and keep adding around: the first circle having six motifs, the second having 12, and so on.

9. For fringe: There are 612 fringes in this design, equaling 3.366 yards (3.08 m). Knot the fringe in CH 3 loops, in CH 5 loops, in CH 3 loops on each point, and where points join in CH 3 loop over 3 DC, in joined points, in CH 3 loop over 3 DC.

10. You can translate these motifs into other materials quite easily. You may want to try knit-crosheen and a slightly bigger hook, or 4-ply yarn and a size F hook, for a blanket instead of a tablecloth.

**Christmas Crafts
Year-Round**

*C*hristmas
Stockings

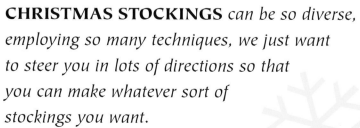

CHRISTMAS STOCKINGS *can be so diverse, employing so many techniques, we just want to steer you in lots of directions so that you can make whatever sort of stockings you want.*

Materials

- various stocking bases
- yarns and ribbons
- beads and beadwork
- fringes
- metallic threads
- embroidery floss
- braids and trims
- fabric glue

Tools

- basic sewing tools
- a marking pen

Instructions

1. Either find a stocking, or make one your-self—either out of purchased fabric or some you've woven yourself.

2. Your choices for decoration are many, and can utilize all sorts of techniques: weav-ing, loomed beadwork, applique, embroi-dery, cross-stitch, needlepoint, surface design, and even glued-on designs.

3. Use your imagination to create any sort of stocking that might please some special child on your gift list.

Contributing Designers

Metric Conversion Chart

LINEAR MEASUREMENTS

INCHES	CM	INCHES	CM	INCHES	CM
1/8	0.3	9	22.9	30	76.2
1/4	0.6	10	25.4	31	78.7
3/8	1.0	11	27.9	32	81.3
1/2	1.3	12	30.5	33	83.8
5/8	1.6	13	33.0	34	86.4
3/4	1.9	14	35.6	35	88.9
7/8	2.2	15	38.1	36	91.4
1	2.5	16	40.6	37	94.0
1 1/4	3.2	17	43.2	38	96.5
1 1/2	3.8	18	45.7	39	99.1
1 3/4	4.4	19	48.3	40	101.6
2	5.1	20	50.8	41	104.1
2 1/2	6.4	21	53.3	42	106.7
3	7.6	22	55.9	43	109.2
3 1/2	8.9	23	58.4	44	111.8
4	10.2	24	61.0	45	114.3
4 1/2	11.4	25	63.5	46	116.8
5	12.7	26	66.0	47	119.4
6	15.2	27	68.6	48	121.9
7	17.8	28	71.1	49	124.5
8	20.3	29	73.7	50	127.0

Index of Projects